WENDY HILL

ON THE SURFACE

THREAD EMBELLISHMENT & FABRIC MANIPULATION

 PUBLISHING

Editor: Liz Aneloski
Technical Editor: Sally Lanzarotti
Copy Editor: Judith Moretz
Cover Designers: Kathy Lee and John Cram
Design Director: Diane Pedersen
Book Designer: Riba Taylor
Illustrator: Richard Sheppard
Photographer: Steve Buckley, Photographic Reflections
Photo Stylist: Ann Sanderson

Library of Congress Cataloging-in-Publication Data

Hill, Wendy,
    On the Surface : thread embellishment and fabric
manipulation / Wendy Hill.
        p.   cm.
    Includes index.
    ISBN 1-57120-032-0
    1. Fancy work.   2. Machine sewing.   3. Texture
(Art)   4. Textile design.   I. Title.
    TT751.H55   1997
    746—dc21
                            97-12599
                            CIP

Published by C&T Publishing, Inc., P.O. Box 1456,
Lafayette, California 94549

Printed in Hong Kong
10 9 8 7 6 5 4 3 2 1

DEDICATION

To my grandmother
Eva Bortle Matthews,

I must make my creation
good and honest and true
with hands and heart and mind
so that it may speak for me after
    I am gone,
telling others something of
    the pleasure I found in its making.
Then my creation will be art
for my work will have been done honestly
    and lovingly,
in the realization of my vision.

ACKNOWLEDGMENTS

This book is the result of the combined efforts of many people and
companies. Thank you, thank you everyone who helped me become an
author of my very own book. A special nod goes to the local fabric stores
in my old hometowns of Nevada City and Grass Valley, California, who
have encouraged and helped me in my transition from public school-
teacher to quilt teacher. They are Heidi's Fabrics, The Quilt Loft,
Fabrications, and U.S. Sewing Machines. The students willing to spend
time and money taking a Wendy Hill class also deserve recognition.
Thank you students everywhere, every age, who in turn, teach the teacher.

To all the contributors, your work makes this book shine. Thank you
also Ann Sanderson for your professional fiddling, gifted eye, and tricks
of the trade, and to Kelly Simbirdi, who generously volunteered to be
my "monkey" (she knows what this means).

Please give a round of applause to my husband and son. Thank you,
David, for months of delicious dinners, and Lucas, for hanging out in
my studio after school, and all the other ways you have both helped.
Let's celebrate!

Caroline's Coffee Roasters and The Peacock Inn, both of Grass Valley,
California, generously allowed camera and crew to invade during hectic
business hours for location photography. Thank you, thank you.

Don't stop reading yet. The following companies generously gave me
materials to make the projects and samples found in this book. I hope
they all will be as pleased as I am with the results. Please see the
Resources on page 141 for more information.

American Effird Incorporated	Hoffman California Fabrics
Bernina of America	Linda Lee of The Sewing Workshop
Bend Vac & Sew	Collection
Coats & Clark	Madeira Division, SCS/USA
Euro-Notions	Sulky of America
Gutermann of America, Inc.	YLI Corporation

CONTENTS

INTRODUCTION
AND HOW TO USE THIS BOOK

Surface stitching is deceptively simple, yet it appears to be sophisticated and difficult to achieve. Until now, how to embellish with thread, without free-motion techniques where you drop the feed dogs, has largely been a mystery. But with this book you'll see just how easy it is to create wonderfully textured surface-stitched clothing, quilts, and all sorts of things with just a straight stitch, leaving the feed dogs up and the sewing machine set for normal stitching.

This book is about texture and design, two elements used in quiltmaking today and in the past. In addition to piecing and appliqué, you'll discover related ways to manipulate a fabric surface using whole cloth, raw-edge collage, and weaving techniques and how to create texture using surface stitching.

If you meet the three criteria below, I promise you'll be able to surface stitch too:

1. You must be conscious. There's just no getting around it—you must be able to sit up at the sewing machine and make it go.

2. The sewing machine must be able to sew a straight stitch. Stitching forward is required; reverse is handy, but optional. This includes all machines—hand crank (or just cranky), treadle, and fancy electric models. (It may be beneficial to zigzag for raw-edge collage.)

3. You must have some time—entry level sewing skills, but time. The resulting color and texture is worth every minute, and it's actually fun to watch the layers of thread color build up until the texture feels just about right.

In the following pages I'll share all I know about surface stitching using the "classic Wendy Hill" method. Chapters 1 and 2 provide the knowledge base for creating projects using surface stitching. Chapters 3, 4, and 5 expand your

options with manipulating the fabric surface using whole cloth, raw-edge collage, and weaving, and Chapter 6 gives you the nitty-gritty of surface stitching. Chapter 7 offers encouragement with starter projects and inspirational samples made by me and former students.

Please take the time to read the acknowledgments on page 2. I discovered it takes a "village" to write a book. Read about the contributors on page 140—people a lot like you in one way or another. And check out the resource section on page 141 for related products and where to find them.

My classes serve as a starting point, and so does this book. I give you the tools you need to take this technique and run with it. Pick up where I've left off and start making your own beautiful surface-stitched fabric to use in quilts, clothing, or anything else you dare to imagine.

Chapter 1
GETTING STARTED

SURFACE STITCHING

The surface stitching presented in this book developed over time into what could be called "classic Wendy Hill" surface stitching. It begins with a fabric surface, which may be manipulated first. The fabric surface is then covered with multiple layers of straight stitching, using a regular presser foot with the feed dogs in the normal up position on the sewing machine (absolutely no free-motion stitching). The various kinds and colors of thread are distributed evenly, using different stitch styles to achieve the desired density. When washed and dried, the surface-stitched fabric is uniquely crinkly and textured.

This simple basic technique may be applied in many ways. The fabric surface can be one piece of fabric (surface stitched to add texture and interest) or manipulated first, then surface stitched. Try piecing or appliquéing a whole-cloth surface, or use raw-edge collage or weaving to make a new surface before surface stitching.

Note: In quiltmaking the term "whole cloth" is used to mean one piece of fabric. In this book the term whole cloth is expanded to include any method of piecing or appliqué to create one complete surface.

You can also use surface stitching to make reversible clothing or quilts in one easy step. With this application the surface stitching is sewn through all the layers at once. Clothing is then assembled using raw-edge construction methods, with overlapped, sometimes covered seams and binding, while quilts are bound around the outside edges.

CHOOSING FABRICS

The basic rule for choosing fabrics is to select those which will perform according to your needs. In order to get the crinkly texture, the fabric must be washed and dried after the surface stitching is complete, so the first general criteria for most projects is to choose washable fabrics.

The next general criteria is related to the need for drape or stiffness. In general, clothing and bed quilts need to drape, while wall quilts need to have some stiffness to hang flat. Choose fabrics accordingly. Keep in mind that the surface stitching, as well as each added fabric layer, will make the piece stiffer. (see Creating a Fabric Surface, beginning on page 23)

TIP

If you fall in love with a light-weight fabric that drapes, but need more stiffness, layer it with muslin for added weight before surface stitching. (Do not use fusible interfacing or it will not shrink and crinkle as you want it to.)

FIBER CONTENT

Experiments I did with surface-stitched fabrics revealed about the same amount of shrinkage with cotton, cotton/polyester blends, polyester, rayon, silk, and taffeta fabrics, but the cotton fabrics looked the most textured after washing and drying. (see Prewashing and Shrinking, page 17) Thick fabrics, such as denim, corduroy, or heavy flannel, don't crinkle very much, but the stitched thread sits nicely on top of the fabric. The thread disappears in fabrics with deep pile, such as polar fleece or velvet. Let the look you desire determine the fabrics you choose.

COLOR COMBINATIONS

The layers of thread in surface stitching have a magical effect on the fabrics, pulling together and unifying even the most disparate colors. It is very difficult to go wrong with surface stitching, but we all have our own color sensibilities. The subject of color and value is complex and there are a number of good books you can refer to for valuable information about color theory. In the meantime, I have assembled some color guidelines I think are useful:

- Try ignoring preconceptions about the colors you love and hate. Surprise yourself with new color combinations you never dreamed of using before.

- Let the fabrics speak to you. One fabric by itself is limited in what it can "say." Is the group of fabrics together a babble of voices (disconnected), a conversation (flowing but somewhat disconnected), or a melody (flowing and connected)?

- Look for those *dissonant* or *accent* fabrics which, when used in small amounts, bring the rest of the fabrics to life. It might take courage at first, but you'll love the results.

A lucky few are born with an innate sense of color. The rest of us must work at it. Learn by observing the wealth of color combinations around you, including those found in nature, department store displays, advertisements, yarn stores, the fish market, or any other place you find yourself.

To help imagine what a group of fabrics will look like when cut up and placed together, look through one of the gadgets which imitates the vision of a fly. I call them "bug-eye lenses." They come with different configurations on the lenses, including triangles, hexagons, squares, and more. Aim it at the bolts of fabric at the store, and you'll see the different fabrics side by side, as if cut up and mixed together.

Collecting fabrics.
Note "bug eye" lenses.

COLLECTING THREADS

The two broad categories of thread are utility and decorative. Utility thread is designed to perform a function, primarily to sew a seam smoothly and strongly. Decorative threads are meant to lie on top of the fabric. When sewing, match the fiber content of the thread to the job it must perform. In surface stitching the thread's job is to lie on top of the fabric, and it must hold up in the washer and dryer, so both utility and decorative threads may be used.

Utility and decorative thread can be described by its thickness, flexibility, and surface texture. A look at each of these qualities is helpful when deciding what kind of thread to purchase.

Thread is manufactured in different thicknesses, or sizes, ranging from size 30 to 100. The smaller the number, the thicker the thread, with standard thread size being 50. Regular embroidery and topstitching threads are thicker, in the 30–40 size range. Fine embroidery, lingerie, and bobbin threads are finer, in the 60–100 range. Any size thread can be used for surface stitching as long as it will go through the sewing machine; in fact, using a mix of thicker and thinner threads is a way to alter the appearance of the texture.

Thread flexibility is related to its fiber content, with some fibers being naturally more flexible, such as polyester, cotton/poly blends, and silk. Mercerized cotton is more flexible than non-mercerized cotton thread.

Surface texture of the thread is more related to the manufacturing process. Thread made from short fibers tends to be less consistent in diameter, more slubby, and produces a lot of lint. Long fiber threads are generally more consistent in diameter, stronger, and more lustrous. Thread can be spun, extruded, or air textured, all of which can affect the quality of the thread.

Buy good quality, reputable brands of thread, and let experience with the thread's performance in your machine guide you. The brochures provided free by the manufacturer contain helpful information.

THE PROS AND CONS OF THREAD FIBER CONTENT

Following is a quick discussion of the many different kinds of thread available to us today. But even the wise consumer will have trouble keeping up with the manufacturing processes of various brands of thread, because the technology is constantly changing. A good rule of thumb is to buy good quality, reputable name brand thread. Thread is about 80 percent moisture when it comes from the factory; over time it will become brittle, so use it before it dries out.

COTTON

Cotton thread is smooth, soft, and flexible, but it has little stretch. Cotton threads are usually mercerized for added strength, preshrunk, and may be treated in other ways to make them more glossy or lustrous. Hand quilting thread is usually waxed, and shouldn't be used in the sewing machine, unless specifically approved by the manufacturer.

Cotton thread breaks more easily than other threads, and when made from short staple fibers, it produces more lint. Over a long period of time cotton thread will break down and begin to disintegrate. It is available in a wide variety of colors and thicknesses. It resists untwisting, and causes less drag when running through the sewing machine mechanism. Surface stitching with cotton thread gives a soft look.

POLYESTER

Polyester thread is strong and elastic. It can be made from short fibers or longer filaments. Good quality polyester threads are consistently uniform in thickness and smoothness, with very few flaws from one spool to the next. It comes glossy or flat in appearance and is available in many colors.

Polyester thread leaves more lint in the bobbin case and tension discs than other fiber contents, and it tends to untwist and stretch in the sewing machine mechanism. Surface stitching with polyester thread can give either a soft look, if a flat, non-reflective thread is used, or a lustrous look, if a glossy thread is used.

COTTON/POLY BLENDS

Often called "all purpose," cotton-wrapped polyester threads have both the strength of polyester and the smooth heat-resistant surface of cotton. Good quality blended threads provide the best of both worlds. A poor quality blend will give you a stretchy thread with an uneven surface, and a host of headaches in the sewing machine mechanism. Use the correct size needle with cotton/poly blends to avoid stripping the outer cotton thread layer from the polyester core.

RAYON

Sometimes known as "poor man's silk," rayon thread is made from wood shavings. Despite coming from a natural product, it is considered to be man-made. Rayon thread is shiny, washable (don't use bleach), and comes in a wide variety of beautiful colors, since it takes dye so well. It loses strength when washed, so it can't

be used as a utility thread. Overall, it breaks more easily than other fibers and has a tendency to slip off the spool and wrap itself around the spindle during sewing. Use all-rayon threads for a very reflective, lustrous surface, or mix rayon threads with other fibers as an accent in the overall surface stitching.

SILK

Silk threads, made from long filaments, is strong, elastic, and has a smooth luster. Its slippery surface glides through fabric when hand sewing. Some brands may not be washable, so check this before purchasing. Silk is expensive, and can be hard to find, but is wonderful to work with. If it is not available in your local stores, look for mail-order sources.

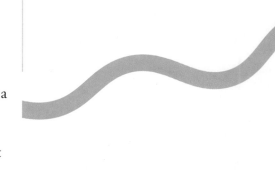

NYLON

Monofilament thread is the best known nylon thread in the sewing world. Made from a complex organic molecule, monofilament comes in two sizes, but be sure to use only the finest, .004, in your sewing machine. Available in clear and smoke, it is inexpensive, strong, and washable.

Nylon thread tends to slip off the spool and wrap around the spindle. Some people believe it can damage the tension discs of the sewing machine, and it can rot when left in direct sunlight over a period of time. When texture without any color is desired, use nylon thread for surface stitching. I use monofilament thread as the top thread of the sewing machine only.

METALLICS

Metallic threads are available in many different thicknesses and styles, including the flat ribbon style. The surface appearance varies from thin and wiry, to glossy, fuzzy, and holographic. The current metallic threads are easier to work with than ever before; however, they still require some special handling. Metallic threads can fray, break easily, and might leave harsh lint in the tension discs and bobbin case of the sewing machine. To minimize problems, use sewing machine needles especially designed for metallic threads. A small amount of metallic thread in the thread mix adds a subtle accent or use more for all-out glitz.

OTHER

In the decorative thread category you will find wool/acrylic blends, all acrylic, neon polyesters, and other novelty threads. These can be difficult to find; you might want to ask your local retailer about other kinds of threads made by the same manufacturers the store regularly carries.

There are a variety of useful utility threads which perform specific functions. For example, fusible thread can be used in the bobbin; when ironed, the thread fuses the seam, such as a hem. For basting, regular basting thread is economical, but must be removed by hand. Water soluble basting thread melts away in the wash, making it very convenient for surface stitching, because there is no need to tediously pick out the basting thread trapped under layers of surface stitching.

SELECTING THREADS FOR SURFACE STITCHING

In theory, any mix of thread fiber content works for surface stitching. In practice, think about the look you want to achieve with your project. Pick flat, glossy, or reflective threads according to your needs, using all of the above on occasion. For example, metallic threads are fun to use, but they don't belong in every project. On the flip side, sometimes reflective and shiny threads are a great addition, so don't be afraid to use them.

Multiple layers of thread resulting in closely spaced stitching lines is the secret to getting the fabulous overall look and texture of surface-stitched fabric. The number of spools required is related to both the assortment of colors and the size of the project. Classic Wendy Hill surface stitching uses ten to twenty different colors of threads in any given project, and the equivalent of about ten full 250 yard spools of thread for a vest. For your first projects, take advantage of your leftover spools of thread and fabrics from your stash. You may find it easier to begin with cotton or cotton/poly thread. Chances are good you'll come to love surface stitching and will begin a thread stash along with your fabric collection.

MAKING FRIENDS WITH YOUR SEWING MACHINE

All sewing machines, old and new, perform the same basic functions with the needle, thread, and bobbin. However, it wouldn't be accurate to say nothing much has changed in the last hundred years. Since their invention, new technologies have continued to improve the stitch quality and performance abilities of sewing machines.

The next time you want to throw your machine out the window, think about the very first sewing machine. It used a looper instead of a bobbin to form a chain stitch, and it could only sew a few inches before the thread broke. Yet this inconvenience didn't stop women from wanting the latest technology available.

Surface stitching makes a different kind of demand on your sewing machine than clothing, quilt-making, and other construction sewing. The machine can be run continuously until the bobbin thread runs out, dulling the needle and filling the bobbin case with lint in no time at all. Be careful not to overheat your sewing machine. Stop and rest to allow the machine to cool off. Speaking with the voice of experience, I recommend you learn to make friends with your sewing machine. You'll both be happier during your hours of surface stitching together.

STRONG EVEN STITCHES

Today's machines, with a bobbin and a lock stitch, are capable of stitching a continuous seam for hours and hours, if we make sure the needle, thread, and machine are all working together. Good performance depends on many factors under our control, including becoming educated about our machine, keeping our machine well maintained, using proper threading, adjusting the tension correctly, and choosing the correct needle for the thread and fabric.

EDUCATION

Take some time to learn all you can about your sewing machine. All machines may seem basically alike, but each have their own features— and quirks. Review the sewing machine manual from time to time and use your local sewing machine dealer as a resource, for formal classes and informal chatting, to achieve the best stitch possible.

MAINTENANCE

Proper and frequent maintenance is a high priority in keeping your sewing machine humming along. At home, clean and oil the machine every two to four hours of surface stitching. Use a soft cloth or brush (never metal tools) to clean the lint that accumulates in surprising quantities under the feed dogs and stitch plate, around the bobbin case, and inside the hook race. Oil the machine according to the directions included with your sewing machine using good quality sewing machine oil. Use canned air to blow across the tension discs where lint and thread fragments can accumulate. Follow up your home maintenance with regular maintenance from your local dealer at least once a year, or more often if you are doing a lot of sewing and surface stitching.

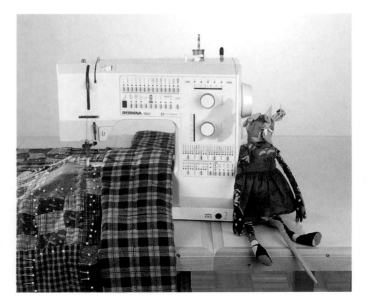

PROPER THREADING

Properly threading the machine is an important step in improving the stitch quality of your machine. Place the thread on the spindle so the thread feeds away from the notch found on many types of spools. Raise the presser foot prior to threading the machine; this opens up and allows the thread to get in all the way between the tension discs. Make sure the thread clicks into place along the way, especially in slotted take-up levers. Thread the needle in the direction specified by the manufacturer, keeping the thread from twisting as you thread the needle. Be sure the bobbin is filled and inserted correctly, with the bobbin rotating in the proper direction.

TENSION

Optimal thread tension means the stitch will form correctly, and the knot will be concealed between the two fabric layers, in the hole made by the needle. Poor tension results in surface knots, loose loops, or thread breakage, and on bad days, all three in rapid succession. Raised knots on the bottom of the fabric means the upper thread tension is too loose; knots on the top of the fabric means it is too tight. Refer to your sewing machine manual when adjusting the tension.

Keeping a record of tension settings for the different threads and fabrics you use may help maintain your sanity.

The bobbin tension is set at the factory, and most sewing machine mechanics do not advise trying to reset it yourself. Classic Wendy Hill surface stitching does not require any special bobbin tension, but some thread embellishment techniques do. Before experimenting with different bobbin tensions, seek advice or take a class from your local dealer.

THE RIGHT NEEDLE

There are two things to remember about needles: choose the right needle and change it often. Needles come in different varieties and sizes to accommodate the thread, fabric, and type of sewing. When sewing, the thread lies in the groove of the needle and fits through the eye in the point. If the needle is too small, the thread can't fit in the groove or will be squeezed through the eye, causing the familiar fraying of the thread; too big, and the thread swims through the groove and eye, causing loops and breakage.

Almost all home sewing machines use system 130/705H, which refers to the length, diameter, and point of the needle. The size of the needle is given first in metric and then in United States equivalent measurements. For example, an 80/12 needle is 80 metric and 12 in the U.S. equivalent. The smaller the number, the finer the needle, just the opposite of thread. Universal needles come in the widest size range; specialty needles come in limited size ranges.

Needles become blunt, bent, hooked, and brittle over time, and not much time at that. For normal sewing, change the needle every six hours, or two garments, whichever comes first. When surface stitching, which causes more wear and tear on the needle, change the needle every three to four sewing hours. Don't wait to hear the "tick, tick, tick" of a dull needle, or worse, for the needle to break, before changing it. Fresh, sharp needles improve the stitch quality and reduce problems with fraying and breakage—of thread and our tempers.

Choosing the right needle is easier today than ever before. In addition to the familiar universal needles, we have ball point, stretch, quilting, jeans/denim, leather, embroidery, metallic, and topstitching—with more being developed all the time. The specific names of these kinds of needles vary from brand to brand. Often the needle company provides a free brochure of their complete line of needles; ask for one at your local retailer the next time you shop. Below is a brief discussion of these needles.

Universal: Used for standard sewing; the point is slightly rounded, but still sharp. Available in all sizes, they can be easily matched with fabric and thread. For surface stitching, size 80/12 is usually appropriate with standard size utility thread.

Embroidery: These needles have a specially shaped eye to accept rayons and other specialty threads. These needles are wonderful to use when surface stitching.

Metallic: Needles designed for metallic thread has a deeper, more elongated groove and a large eye. The design almost eliminates the dreaded shredding and fraying associated with metallic threads—fantastic news for surface stitching.

Topstitching: Topstitching needles have an extra-large eye and groove to accept thicker thread. Try these needles when surface stitching with thicker threads or when using two threads through the same needle.

Micro: These needles are designed for topstitching silk thread and for sewing with the new microfiber fabrics, such as waterproof fabrics, polar fleece, and ultrasuede. They are extremely sharp, resulting in very straight stitching lines. Try using these needles when surface stitching tightly woven fabrics.

Ball point: These needles have very round points designed for use with girdle-type knit fabrics.

Stretch: The point is not as round as a ball point needle, and it sits closer to the hook when forming a stitch, resulting in fewer or no skipped stitches. They often come with an anti-static coating. Use with knit fabrics.

Quilting: These needles are very sharp with a large eye. They are designed to be used when machine quilting through the layers of the quilt sandwich.

Jeans/denim: These needles are strong, with a larger eye and sharp point. Use for denim and other densely woven, sturdy fabrics.

Other: There are a variety of specialty needles available, such as those just for leather or for doing heirloom sewing. Also, there are double and triple needles, with two or three needles attached to one "stem." I have not used these needles with surface stitching.

TIP

When surface stitching you might switch back and forth between thread types, resulting in needle changes before the life of the needle has expired. Replace the used needles into the package backwards, so you'll know which needles are new and which are used.

ANATOMY OF A STITCH

All current machines make a lockstitch. In essence, a simple knot is created with the top and bobbin threads. A seam could be called a series of knots. In order to understand the importance of proper threading and tension adjustment, let's look at what happens when a stitch is formed. Place an imaginary dot on the thread as it leaves the spool. The dot travels about 23" to a spot just above the eye of the needle.

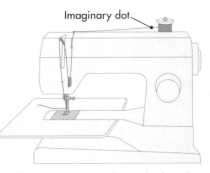

Place an imaginary dot on the thread as it leaves the spool.

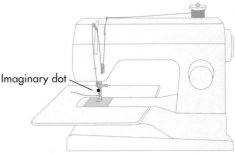

The dot travels about 23" to a spot just above the eye of the needle.

To begin the stitch, the thread comes from the tension discs, the take up lever is all the way up and the needle is in the up position.

The take up lever goes down, and the dot passes through the eye and becomes part of the loop formed in the bobbin case. The hook on the race mechanism swings the bobbin thread around, forming the knot with the loop.

The take up lever goes back up, sucking up the thread in the loop, and our imaginary dot lands just shy of its starting place. The stitch is completed.

This process continues at a frantic pace as stitches are formed, and according to one manufacturer, our dot passes back and forth through the needle about fifty times before coming to rest, at last, in a stitch. With this kind of wear and tear, we need to do all we can to help the machine make a good stitch.

ANATOMY OF A STITCH

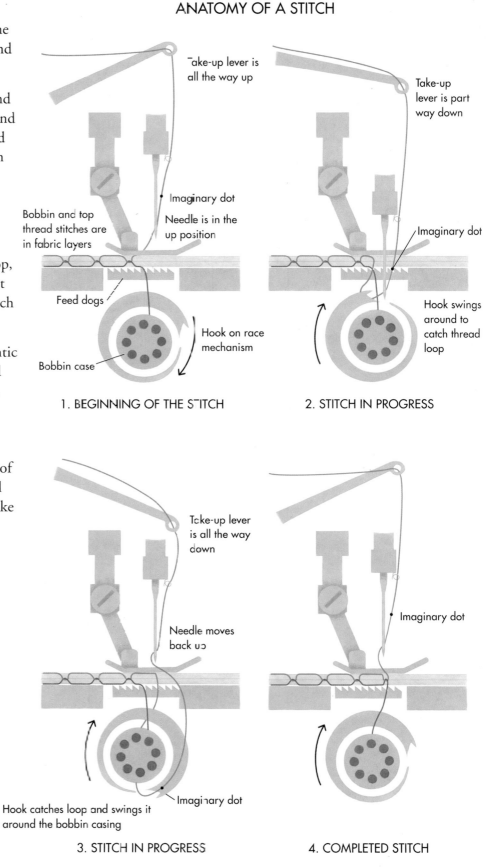

Take-up lever is all the way up

Imaginary dot

Needle is in the up position

Bobbin and top thread stitches are in fabric layers

Feed dogs

Hook on race mechanism

Bobbin case

1. BEGINNING OF THE STITCH

Take-up lever is part way down

Imaginary dot

Hook swings around to catch thread loop

2. STITCH IN PROGRESS

Take-up lever is all the way down

Needle moves back up

Hook catches loop and swings it around the bobbin casing

Imaginary dot

3. STITCH IN PROGRESS

Imaginary dot

4. COMPLETED STITCH

REMINDERS & TROUBLE-SHOOTING

▪ Frequently clean and oil the sewing machine. Blow canned air across the tension discs. This cannot be overstated when surface stitching.

▪ Do not let your machine get too hot. Turn off the machine and take a break.

▪ Select the correct needle, and change it about every three to four hours when surface stitching. Make sure the needle is pushed all the way up into the hole and facing the correct direction when replacing the needle.

▪ Wind the bobbin slowly and evenly (instead of running the pedal to the metal). It will unwind evenly, too. Likewise, sew with an even speed across the surface of the fabric. Be sure the thread is feeding off the bobbin in the correct direction.

▪ If the thread is unwinding and wrapping onto the spindle, switch to a vertical spindle if your machine offers this option (or horizontal, depending on what you started with). If this doesn't work, place the spool of thread into a narrow jar (so the thread can't topple over) and feed the thread into the sewing machine through a paper clip taped to the machine, above and to the side of the handwheel.

▪ Take the time to thread the sewing machine carefully, listening for the thread to "click" into all the correct places, such as a slotted take-up lever. Make sure the bobbin is inserted correctly.

▪ If you just can't get the machine to behave and sew a good stitch without tension problems or thread breakage, turn off the machine and give both it and you a rest. If problems persist, check your owner's manual or consult with a sewing machine service person.

ASSEMBLING THE ESSENTIALS

In addition to fabric and thread, there are a few supplies and tools which are very useful for surface stitching.

Water soluble glue stick, water soluble basting thread, and water soluble stabilizer: These are not absolutely necessary, but they sure make surface stitching easier when manipulating the fabric surface, securing the layers, and stitching. They all wash out of the fabric during the washing and drying step, eliminating bulk and the need to pick out basting. Look for water soluble glue stick brands which say "washes out" (not "washable"), such as Avery Disappearing Color Glue Stic®, and Avery Permanent Glue Stic® and

water soluble stabilizer under the brand names Solv-It™ by YLI, Solvey™ by Sulky, and Avalon® by Madeira.

Low-loft batting: This thin batting makes a good middle layer when you want a little loft in your surface-stitching project.

Quilter's flannel and muslin: These are products usually found in quilt-oriented fabric stores. The flannel is white and meant to be used as a middle layer. The muslin is lightweight, usually wrinkle resistant, and relatively inexpensive.

Extra bobbins: These are convenient to accommodate the variety of thread colors used in a project. Also, leftover bobbins of thread for one project may be saved and

used for another when you have extra bobbins.

Quilter's pins: These are longer than regular pins and usually have a colored head. They are easy to handle and are long enough to go through all the layers.

Masking tape: It is good to have on hand for securing fabric to a flat surface, marking sewing lines on the fabric, and more. Do not leave masking tape on the fabric for an extended period of time or the adhesive may remain on the fabric, leaving a mark.

Walking foot: It is not required for surface stitching, but when stitching through thicker layers this foot makes it easier to stitch the first few layers of thread to prevent tucks and pleats from appearing on the surface of the fabric.

Quilt or bicycle clips: These metal bands are useful when packaging a quilt for surface stitching. Roll up the sides of the quilt, leaving an area for stitching, and secure with the clips.

Fabric marker: Many fabric markers are available, including everything from chalk to washable pens. Choose your favorite washable marker to use with surface stitching.

Rotary cutter, mat, and clear, gridded ruler: These are almost a given these days. It is possible to make the things in this book without these tools, but it is faster to do some kinds of cutting and measuring with these tools.

Maintenance and cleaning tools: These include a soft cloth, a nylon brush, canned air, and a good quality sewing machine oil.

Plastic sandwich bag and trash bag: Tape the plastic sandwich bag to the work table next to the machine for all the thread snips that can be used in other projects (see page 134 for Button Babies and Eraser Head doll pins). Scoop lint and other trimmings into the trash bag as you sew to avoid big clean-up jobs later on.

PLANNING AHEAD

This book is meant to keep you from having to reinvent the wheel, and describes how to get the look found in classic Wendy Hill surface stitching. This open-ended technique is readily adaptable to any project you want to make. You'll be able to achieve this look, but with experimentation you'll also be able to adjust any of the steps according to your own needs and preferences. A little planning ahead will help you target what you need to do for your project.

PREWASHING AND SHRINKING

My experience has shown that surface stitched fabrics always shrink, regardless of the fiber content of the thread and fabric, or whether or not the fabrics have been prewashed. Always allow for shrinkage ahead of time by adding extra fabric before cutting and surface stitching. For clothing and other items using pattern pieces, allow a generous 2" all the way around the cutting line. Large panels of fabric, such as a quilt or large piece of whole cloth, shrink more along the lengthwise grain than the crosswise grain. Allow about 2" for every 45" in width, and 3" for every yard in length. If an exact size is important, allow even more to avoid disappointment.

SELECTING CLOTHING, QUILTS, AND OTHER PATTERNS

The important advice here is to choose a pattern well within your sewing ability. Sometimes it is enough simply to admire a complicated pattern, but save our sanity and self-esteem by choosing a project we can finish. Surface stitching will make anything look more complicated and sophisticated, and it is often the simple styles which stand out anyway.

When choosing a project, remember that surface stitching used in small amounts can be very effective. Look for patterns with yokes, bodies, or other component parts which can be surface stitched. It is not necessary to commit to surface stitching new fabric for an entire garment or quilt. For projects where only a few areas are surface stitched, any pattern will work, because the project will be constructed following the pattern instructions, just as you would for any fabric.

Surface stitching can be used to make a completely reversible garment (such as a simple vest) in one step using raw-edge construction techniques to assemble the garment. The outer edges can then be finished with seam binding. Look for patterns with straight seams, no darts, and no set-in pockets. Also look for simple patterns without small pieces and numerous seams when making clothing using raw-edge collage or weaving. Larger expanses of raw-edge collage and weaving enhance the effect of surface stitching.

Any quilt pattern or design can be used with surface stitching. One way is to make the quilt as usual, but surface stitch rather than quilt, through all the layers. Make new surface-stitched fabric to use in your next quilt, or surface stitch individual blocks prior to assembling the quilt. With advance planning, quilts may be put together using raw-edge collage and weaving.

SPECIAL LAYOUTS

Sometimes it is more convenient and effective to cluster pattern pieces together to make one big shape to surface stitch. For example, clustering two cuffs and a collar into a big rectangle speeds up the surface stitching process and leads to more consistency in the look of the stitching among the separate pieces.

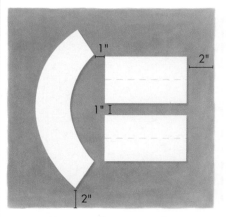

Cluster small pieces together.

For shrinkage, allow 1" between the pieces and 2" all the way around the outside edges of the pieces.

Patterns can be simplified by overlapping pattern seams before cutting out the pieces. If the back of a shirt or jacket has a straight center back seam, overlap the seam

By Heather Braley, Dress with Surface Stitched Bodice (See page 106)

along the center back seamlines to make one big piece. A cuff might be given in two pieces; overlap the seam to make one continuous piece. Another place to overlap seams is at the side or shoulder seams. For example, for a vest or jacket, first trace an extra front pattern piece on paper, then overlap the pieces to make one big unit for the two fronts and the back. This gives you one big design surface, eliminates a step in constructing the garment later, and makes it easier to surface stitch.

Overlap seam allowances
to create one pattern.

When fabric is densely surface stitched with a muslin or flannel backing, it no longer responds to a grainline. This means it can be cut any which way, allowing us to take advantage of a print, design motif, or plaid. Do not try this with just one layer of surface-stitched fabric; it will respond to its grainline by stretching.

Special effects can be created in the layout stage by strategically placing raw-edge or appliquéd designs in fun places, then surface stitching. For example, when making a garment with buttons, place fun shapes over the spots where the buttonholes will be. Or add "fussy cut" motifs from fabrics along the hem or on the pocket of pieces which will be surface stitched.

Quilt patterns based on a grid design are adaptable to raw-edge techniques. First, change your thinking about the way quilt tops are constructed starting with units

Fussy Cut Motifs

and proceeding to blocks, rows, and finally the whole top. Instead, think of the quilt top as a whole. A layout grid is created on muslin or flannel, and the grid blocks are simply filled in with the component pieces. Use this special layout with watercolor-type quilts, nine-patch designs, and other grid quilt designs. (Refer to Chapter 4, page 41, for marking layout grids, and page 82 and page 90 for projects using layout grids.)

Layout Grid

Raw edges overlapped for "pieced look"

SOMETIMES
A GREAT NOTION

Anything can be made a little more fun, sophisticated, or professional looking with the simple addition of the right button, trim, fastener, binding, cording, or other embellishment.

Look for the right button to accent your clothing, or plan an entire garment around a special button. Cover buttons with surface-stitched fabric for an added bit of texture and color.

Look for handmade buttons made of polymer clay or other materials. Replace the buttons on a purchased garment, transforming it into a one-of-a-kind wearable art piece.

Instead of a button for a fastener, look in all sorts of places for unlikely but fascinating closures. Try junk jewelry, miniature ornaments, ribbon roses, wooden shapes, earrings, rings, and more.

With a little extra (but not much) effort, add trims, bindings, and cordings. Make your own bias trim and cording with matching fabrics, or look for purchased trims,

cording, and laces. Try putting neck and sleeve facings on the right side of the garment to take advantage of a bias-cut plaid or contrasting fabric. Add bias trim over seams. Instead of hemming, add a contrasting hem (stitch right side of contrasting hem fabric to wrong side of garment) to show on the right side. Sew cording or flat trim into seams. Rattail cording can be attached with monofilament thread using an open zigzag stitch. Imagination is more important than sewing skill, and these small additions make your work stand out as unique; just smile and accept the compliments without revealing your secrets.

SUMMARY

Surface stitching and fabric manipulation are very accessible techniques for everyone, from the beginner to the experienced sewer or quiltmaker. Follow my instructions and you will be amazed with the endless possibilities; but remember to tackle patterns within your sewing ability. For your first projects, try using fabrics from your stash and leftover spools of thread. You don't need any special materials or tools to get started. Remember to be friends with your sewing machine for many happy hours of stitching. Before starting a project, refresh your memory and refer to the Planning Ahead section on page 17. Then read on with confidence, knowing you can make a beautiful surface-stitched "treasure" in the near future.

Chapter 2
THE BASIC TECHNIQUE

GETTING THE BIG PICTURE

This chapter will act as a master guide for information about the basic technique. It will cover the three basic steps to create any surface-stitched piece. First, a fabric surface is prepared or created. Next, multiple layers of thread are straight stitched over the surface. Finally, the surface-stitched piece is machine washed and dried. Chapter 3 goes into detail about manipulating the fabric surface with whole cloth, Chapter 4 discusses raw-edge collage, and Chapter 5 gives the process of using weaving to create a fabric surface. Then, Chapter 6 gives you surface-stitching instructions.

CREATING A FABRIC SURFACE

Of the three basic steps, creating the fabric surface involves the most decisions. Focusing on the desired end result of the project helps the choices become clear and easy to make. This section will discuss how to decide on the number of layers needed to achieve the desired drape or stiffness and how to secure these layers.

NUMBER OF LAYERS

The project you choose may require one, two, three, or more layers to be stacked, secured, and possibly zigzag stitched prior to surface stitching. The surface stitching can go through just the top layer or through all layers (top layer, optional batting, backing). To determine the number of layers for any project, answer this question: How much drape or flexibility is required? All other decisions flow from the answer to this question. For example, a shirt or dress and a cuddly lap quilt may require soft flexibility, while a jacket may need to be sturdy, and a wall quilt firm enough to hang flat without drooping.

Use the following chart and flex scale as a guide in making the decisions required to prepare or create the fabric surface. Since the flex scale is based on basic cotton fabrics and low-loft batting, the rating is given as a range to reflect the possible extremes of actual materials.

Flex Scale

1: fragile
2: extremely drapey
3: medium drape
4: somewhat firm
5: firm
6: downright stiff

The top layer can be whole cloth, raw-edge collage, or weaving. The middle layer can be muslin, flannel, or low-loft batting. The bottom layer can be muslin, flannel, or fashion fabric. With three or more layers, the combinations are endless.

Layers	Whole Cloth	Raw-Edge Collage	Weaving
One Layer	Use one piece of fabric or a constructed fabric surface, with or without a wash away stabilizer base.	Use raw-edge shapes with a water soluble stabilizer base.	Not possible.
	Flex Scale: 2 to 4, with pieced surfaces and heavier fabrics having less drape.	*Flex Scale:* 1 to 3, depending on the density of the shapes covering the surface.	
Two Layers	Whole cloth or a constructed top over a base* or fashion fabric for reversibility.	Raw-edge shapes over a base* or a fashion fabric for reversibility.	Two fabrics woven together, variety of fabric strips in warp and weft, one whole cloth base with all or part woven with strips, etc. with or without a water soluble stabilizer base.
	Flex Scale: 3 to 5, with pieced tops and heavier fabrics having less drape.	*Flex Scale:* 2 to 4, depending on the background fabric and density of the shapes covering the surface.	*Flex Scale:* 1 to 3 for raw-edge strips 3 to 5 for bias strips or tubes.
Three Layers	Same as a two layer project, plus a middle layer**	Same as a two layer project, plus a middle layer.**	Same as a two layer project, plus a middle layer** and/or a base* or fashion fabric for reversibility.
	Flex Scale: 4 to 6	*Flex Scale:* 4 to 6 depending on the middle layer and density of the raw-edge shapes covering the surface.	*Flex Scale:* 4 to 6, depending on the use of raw edges, bias strips, or tubes.

* muslin or flannel   ** muslin, flannel, or low loft batting

STACKING THE LAYERS

Remember, the surface stitching can go through just the top layer or through all layers (top layer, optional batting, backing). Decide on the number of layers, and stack from the bottom up. Once the number of layers has been determined, the layers must be stacked and secured. First the layers are stacked on a flat work surface, similar to layering a quilt for quilting.

TIP

When surface stitching one layer of fabric, layer over water soluble stabilizer for better stitch quality. When using a water soluble stabilizer, the stabilizer is placed on the bottom of the stack.

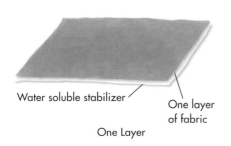

Water soluble stabilizer

One layer of fabric

One Layer

For non-reversible projects, the fabric base is placed first (right or wrong side up; it doesn't matter). The optional middle layer is added next, with the top layer added right side up on the stack.

For reversible pieces, the backing fabric is placed right side down. The optional middle layer is added next, with the top layer added right side up on the stack.

Fabric base—
muslin or flannel

Optional middle layer

Three Layers

Fabric backing

Optional middle layer

Reversible Piece

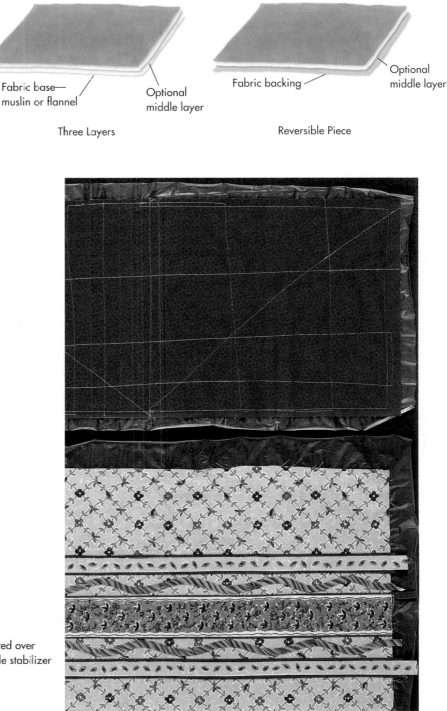

Fabric layered over water soluble stabilizer

SECURING THE LAYERS

Unless the piece is very small, the stack of layers must be secured in some way prior to stitching. Even a medium-sized piece, such as the front of a vest, can shift dramatically as it is stitched with the sewing machine. Visible pleats and tucks created by shifting layers during stitching do not enhance the overall look of the finished piece, so do not try to save time by skipping this step. Remember, if you don't have time to do it right, how will you have time to do it over?

There are several easy and relatively painless ways to secure the layers together:

Pin basting: The long quilter's pins are a good choice for small to medium pieces. Shown are examples of how pins would be placed. The pins may be placed in columns down a whole-cloth piece (about 1½" apart in the column, with columns about 3" apart),

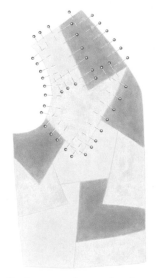

Pinning around raw-edge shapes

around raw-edge shapes (about every ½"), or along woven strips (about every ½"). This method is possible though difficult for larger pieces, since it is time consuming, and the sharp pins tend to poke you while you are sewing (ouch).

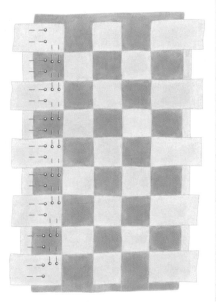

Pinning along woven strips

Water soluble thread: This wonderful product may be used for hand or machine basting. Since it washes out, there is no need to remove the basting later—a definite plus. Use it in the bobbin and top thread of your machine for machine stitching. Be careful when ironing a piece basted with this thread, since hot steam can start the melting process earlier than desired.

Water soluble glue stick: Some glue sticks are made to wash out of children's clothing, which means they can be used to baste and will safely wash out later. This method is good for raw-edge shapes or other projects with smaller areas to be glued.

TIP

Read the labels carefully, and avoid "washable" glue sticks, since this means the glue will not wash out in the wash cycle—just the opposite of what is desired.

Water soluble stabilizer: An easy way to secure the layers is to sandwich the stack with a piece of stabilizer on the top. Place a few pins to hold the sandwich together, then machine baste with water soluble thread. This works well with smaller or fragile projects, especially when pin or hand basting would be extremely tedious. See the photos on page 25.

Pinning Whole Cloth

OPTIONAL ZIGZAGGING

Now that the layers are stacked and secured, and ready for stitching, consider whether the piece needs to have any raw edges zigzagged before surface stitching. If the fabric ravels easily, if the surface stitching will be less dense than usual, or if you prefer a more finished look, zigzagging is probably in order.

To zigzag, use a narrow, open zigzag setting with a blending thread color. Stitch along the raw edges. The zigzagging will blend in unnoticed after the surface stitching is complete and the piece is washed and shrunk.

Zigzagging the raw edges with a blending thread color results in a more finished look after the surface stitching. Instead of zigzagging around each shape, start at one side of the piece and zigzag your way across to the other side. Turn the piece around and zigzag your way back. Continue traveling around, zigzagging a path from one side or place to another, until only isolated spots are left to zigzag. Straight stitch to the remaining spots, zigzag the raw edge, then straight stitch to the next spot, zigzag, and so on, until all the raw edges are zigzagged.

Narrow Zigzag Stitch

Zigzag Raw Edges

The first step, creating a fabric surface, is complete. Now the stacked and secured layers are ready to be surface stitched.

SURFACE STITCHING

This step includes selecting the "thread medleys" and stitch style. Chapter 6 goes into detail about actually surface stitching. Imagine the excitement of watching the colors blend and texture develop as you add layer after layer of thread. If you've ever made bread or homemade fudge, you've experienced that moment when you know, by the feel of it, that the bread is kneaded just about right or the fudge is just about ready to set. The same experience occurs with surface stitching at the moment the fabric begins to feel as though it has just about enough texture.

Zigzagging the Raw Edges

WASHING AND SHRINKING

This is the step which makes the surface-stitched fabric shrink and crinkle. More surface stitching equals more shrinking, and the more the stitching lines cross, the more the piece will shrink. Chapter 6, beginning on page 57, shows some examples.

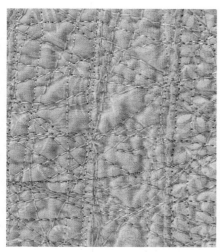

Stitched, Washed, and Dried

THE WASH CYCLE

For most surface-stitched items a regular wash cycle, set for about two minutes, is adequate. If the piece is unusually delicate or fragile, consider a delicate cycle in the washing machine, or hand washing. If you have used a water soluble stabilizer, be aware that a quick hand washing isn't enough to remove all the residue. Any residue left behind leaves the fabric very stiff, as if heavily starched.

If the fabrics have been previously washed, run the washer without any detergent at all. When using unwashed fabrics, use a "dibby dab" of a detergent without any additives. Or try using Orvus WA Paste®, a shampoo meant for horses and whose only ingredient is the same as the main ingredient in human shampoo, sodium lauryl sulfate. It is biodegradable and gentle, yet strong enough to clean an ordinary (no stains) load of wash. A tablespoon of Orvus is enough for a big load of wash; use less for smaller loads. Look for it at your local feed supply store, where it may be purchased economically in assorted size tubs.

A word of caution about using bleach or detergent with special cleaning additives. Rayon and many specialty threads are not meant to be washed with bleach. The colors may run, and some cotton threads may change color. Washing instructions for particular brands of thread are available from the company. Ask for this information at your local store, or contact the company directly.

THE DRYER

The spin cycle will twist and compact your surface-stitched piece. Remove it promptly, then shake or gently pull the surface-stitched item back to its original shape before tossing it into the dryer. It is not advisable to dry surface-stitched (or any) fabric to the bone. This can set in creases and is very stressful for the fiber of the fabric. Instead, set the dryer for very short cycles and keep checking. When the fabric is almost completely dry, take it out, give it a thorough shaking, and allow it to finish drying over an ironing board.

Pressing flattens much of the crinkle, and should be avoided whenever possible. If a surface-stitched item must be pressed, hold the iron just above the surface and press as lightly as possible with steam. Revive flattened crinkle by lightly spraying the surface-stitched piece with water and popping it back into the dryer again for a few minutes.

TIP

When drying a small surface-stitched piece, add some towels to keep the small item moving around the dryer, preventing it from getting stuck over the air vent and possibly catching on fire.

SUMMARY

Sometimes the best features of an open-ended technique also seem like the worst: there are infinite ways to use surface stitching to achieve infinite end results. While inspiring and exciting, this can also seem intimidating and overwhelming. Remember there are just three basic steps to any surface-stitched piece: creating a fabric surface; surface stitching; and washing and drying. Take each step one at a time, and the seemingly impossible becomes a tangible, touchable, fabulous one-of-a-kind surface-stitched piece you can use to create your project.

Chapter 3
WHOLE CLOTH

WHOLE CLOTH METHODS

In quiltmaking, the term "whole cloth" is used to mean one piece of fabric, cut off the bolt. Two or more of these pieces can be seamed together to make one big whole-cloth surface. In this book, the term "whole cloth" is expanded to mean any fabric joined or constructed using any method of piecing or appliqué to create one whole-cloth surface. The fabric can be used right from the bolt (there are certainly enough tempting choices in our local fabric stores), hand-dyed, or painted; or the whole cloth can be pieced or appliquéd.

OFF THE BOLT

Buy printed, woven, or plain fabric off the bolt; or start with a plain fabric and dye, marbleize, paint, air brush, or batik it. Then surface stitch it. This is the easiest way to begin.

CONSTRUCTING THE SURFACE FIRST

Use any kind of piecing or appliquéing method to construct a whole, finished surface (unlike using raw-edge collage or weaving, which I will discuss in Chapters 4 and 5). Try strip piecing, foundation piecing, Victorian crazy quilting, traditional blocks, original designs, charm quilts (using one template shape and one each of different fabrics), appliqué, reverse appliqué, mola techniques— anything and everything which will take pieces of fabric and make them into a whole surface again.

FABRIC ASSORTMENT AND QUANTITY

Although there are no definite rules about which fabrics should be used, the results when using certain fabrics are predictable. Experience is a great teacher, but until then, look closely at the photographs in this book and read the guidelines that follow.

Surface stitching will unify the fabric surface no matter what factors are involved. Solid (or solid in appearance) colored fabrics show off texture more than prints. One piece of fabric directs more attention to the surface stitching than a pieced or appliquéd top layer. When constructing a surface first, keep in mind that designs using low-contrast fabrics tend to blur and loose their distinct look when surface stitched. High-contrast fabrics retain their visibility and contrast with surface stitching.

Take into account that all surface-stitched fabric shrinks. Always allow extra fabric, no matter what you are making. When piecing fabric, you can either make the individual pieces a little bigger and let them shrink, or you can add another row of piecing. For appliqué, plan ahead for the shifting location of the appliqué designs after shrinking.

APPLYING THE BASIC STEPS

Refer to Chapter 1, page 17, to plan ahead for shrinkage and any special cutting layouts. When you select, piece, or appliqué fabric for the surface, refer to Chapter 2, beginning on page 23, to determine the number of layers for your project, the best method to secure the layers, and how to wash and dry your surface-stitched piece. Chapter 6, beginning on page 57, gives you information about how to surface stitch. After you have applied the three basic steps, continue as required to complete your project.

IDEAS

Using a whole-cloth surface is a good way to begin a surface-stitched project. Here are a few ideas to get you started.

Surface stitch fabric to include in an outfit (one layer: fashion fabric with water soluble stabilizer).

Surface stitch a band for a dress (two layers: pieced fashion fabric blocks, muslin).

Surface stitch a reversible vest, with an off-the-bolt print on one side and a solid color on the reverse (three layers: fashion fabric, muslin, fashion fabric).

One layer: fashion fabric with water soluble stabilizer

Two layers: pieced fashion fabric blocks, muslin

Surface stitch a border to use in a quilt top (two layers: fashion fabric, muslin).

Surface stitch fabric for a pieced quilt top; layer and quilt as usual (one layer: fashion fabric with water soluble stabilizer).

Three layers: fashion fabric, muslin, fashion fabric. Modeled by Rachael Ramey.

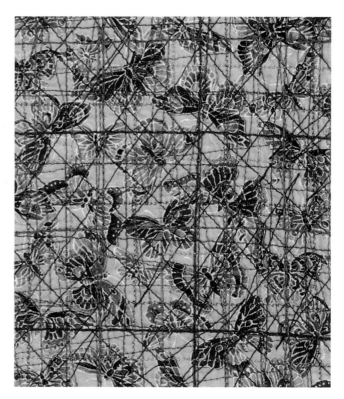

Detail of Vest

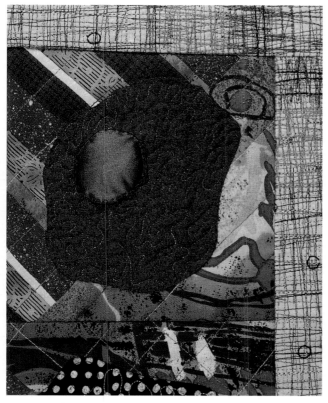

Two layers: fashion fabric, muslin

One layer: fashion fabric with water soluble stabilizer

Three layers: fashion fabric, flannel, fashion fabric

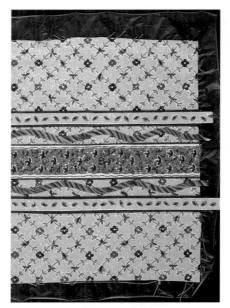

One layer: fashion fabric and ribbons/trims with water soluble stabilizer and decorator fabric with appliqué design

Surface stitch a whole-cloth coverlet (three layers: fashion fabric, flannel, fashion fabric).

Surface stitch ribbons and trims on fabric to make a pillow (one layer: fashion fabric and ribbons/trims with water soluble stabilizer).

Surface stitch an appliquéd pillow top (one layer: heavy decorator fabric with appliqué design).

Surface stitch fabric to make a tote bag or clutch purse (two layers: fashion fabric with muslin base).

Detail of tote bag

Two layers: fashion fabric with muslin base

SPECIAL FEATURE: MIX IT UP

Experiment with new ways to use surface stitching on whole cloth. Try one of these ideas, or think up your own.

■ Try reverse appliqué. You will need two pieces of fabric the same size. Cut shapes out of the top piece of fabric. Layer it over the other piece of whole cloth. The bottom layer of fabric will show through the holes.

■ Use reverse appliqué, but sandwich a third fabric between the layers underneath the cut-out shape, so that the third fabric is seen through the hole.

■ Follow the same idea as above, but save the cut-out shapes. Appliqué the cut-out shapes on the reverse side of a garment or quilt.

■ Try surface stitching just part of a fabric. For example, make a kind of seersucker effect by stitching in vertical bands. The stitched area will shrink unevenly, giving a puckered look.

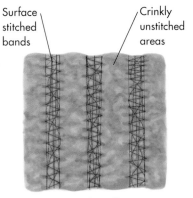

Surface stitched bands

Crinkly unstitched areas

Seersucker effect

Cut out star shape from top layer of fabric.

Bottom layer of fabric

Place top fabric over bottom fabric.

Reverse Appliquéd Stars

Chapter 4

RAW-EDGE COLLAGE

RAW-EDGE COLLAGE METHODS

Another way to manipulate a fabric surface is with the use of raw-edge collage. For the purposes of this text, raw-edge collage is defined as the use of fabric cut into random shapes, geometric shapes, or "fussy cut" motifs from a print fabric, leaving the edges raw (unfinished). As implied with the word collage, the shapes are scattered over a base, either close together with overlapping edges, or farther apart so the background shows through.

RANDOM SHAPES

Random shapes are irregular and cut freely without using a template or measuring. This is a good way to use odd leftover pieces of fabric. You can cut the shapes with scissors or a rotary cutter and mat, whichever is most comfortable.

Sample Random Shapes

FABRIC ASSORTMENT AND QUANTITY

Look for a variety of colors, values, print sizes, and textures. The surface stitching unites the various fabrics, so the more the merrier when you are collecting the fabrics. When there is not much difference between the fabrics in color, value, or print size, the individual pieces lose their form and design with the surface stitching. This might be just the effect you want, but if you want to be able to see the shapes after surface stitching, you need to start with more contrast among the pieces.

Whether you are making a quilt, piece of clothing, pillow, or some other item, collect at least the equivalent of the amount of fabric required if cutting the pieces from whole cloth. For example, if a vest pattern calls for 1¼ yards of 45"-wide fabric for the front and back, collect at least 1¼ yards of assorted fabrics. Choose water soluble stabilizer, muslin, or fashion fabric for the base depending on desired drape and whether the you want the base fabric to show behind the fabric shapes. Remember to add an extra 2" on all sides of the base fabric to allow for shrinkage.

It helps to cut out the pattern or base to be covered (with the allowance for shrinkage added) in order to decide on the sizes of the random pieces.

Low-contrast fabrics blend together.

High-contrast fabrics stand out.

CUTTING THE SHAPES

When cutting the shapes, cut a variety of sizes from small to large. Of course, small to large is relative to the size of the project. It takes a lot of small pieces to cover a surface, and they get lost when they are surface stitched. Large pieces cover the area faster, but can dominate the surface. Experiment with different size shapes before cutting all the fabrics. Look at the piece from a distance. Finding a happy middle ground comes with experience; give yourself permission to learn along the way—this is the fun part. Cut the shapes with scissors or a rotary cutter and mat, whichever is most comfortable. Handle the shapes with care to prevent fraying.

DISTRIBUTION OF THE SHAPES

For most projects, the shapes are scattered across the base, evenly distributing color, value, and size of the shapes. A useful strategy is to divide the base into sections, then divide the shapes into the same number of piles. For example, a three-piece vest would have four sections: right front; left front; right back; and left back (even when the back is cut in one piece). A quilt could be divided into four quadrants: top left; top right; bottom left; and bottom right. A coat might be divided into six sections: right front; left front; right back; left back; right sleeve; and left sleeve.

Start sorting the shapes into piles equal to the number of sections in the project (four sections, four piles, and so on). For example, pick up all the leaf fabric pieces, and put one in each pile. If there are only three leaf fabric pieces

and four piles, this is okay; just pick up the next group of cut shapes and continue where you left off. This strategy distributes the different fabrics over all the areas of the item you'll be covering, eliminating the frightening discovery that all the red-orange fabrics ended up on the right sleeve and nowhere else.

Sorting Shapes into Piles

Shapes Cut Out

PLACEMENT OF THE SHAPES

To start, take a pile of shapes and a surface to cover (base). This is a time for auditioning the pieces in relation to each other, so don't bother with exact placement or overlapping at this stage; just start scattering the shapes. Move shapes around until you like the position of the pieces. When ready, start putting the pieces in their final position. Some shapes might hang off the edge of the base; trim these after the piece is basted. If overlapping the edges, make sure the shapes completely overlap their neighbor ¼", although if a gaping hole is noticed later, it may be easily covered with another random shape patch. If desired, the background layer can be allowed to show around the shapes.

APPLYING THE BASIC STEPS

Refer to Chapter 1, page 17, to plan ahead for shrinkage and any special cutting layouts. When you collage random shapes for the surface, refer to Chapter 2, beginning on page 23, to determine the number of layers for your project. The shapes can be placed over a water soluble stabilizer, resulting in a very flexible, even fragile, surface-stitched piece. Placed over a fabric base, the piece can be drapey, but more substantial. When used with three layers (the shapes, a middle layer, and a lining), the piece can be firm to stiff. Determine the best method to secure the layers of your surface-stitched piece (Chapter 2, page 26). The shapes shift when handled during sewing, so take the

Positioning the Shapes

time to secure the layers now for more enjoyable sewing later. Chapter 6, beginning on page 57, gives you information about how to surface stitch.

Wash and dry your surface-stitched piece with guidance from Chapter 2, page 29. After you have applied the three basic steps, continue as required to complete your project.

Zigzagging the Edges

First layers of surface stitching

GEOMETRIC SHAPES

Geometric shapes are squares, triangles, rectangles, hexagons, and all the other building blocks of pieced quilt patterns. Any project can be made using quilt designs, including clothing, home decorator items, quilts, and more. Any quilt pattern can be assembled with raw-edge geometric shapes, some are just trickier than others. When piecing and sewing we start with individual units, put the units into blocks, sew the blocks into rows, then assemble the rows. This is not true when using raw-edge assembly; instead, the entire project is created using a different series of steps.

The easiest way to get started is to make a quilt design based on squares. The squares can be left whole, or divided into smaller pieces. For example, divide the square into two rectangles, four small squares, two triangles, or four triangles.

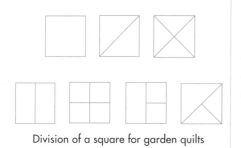

Division of a square for garden quilts

Individual shapes for quilt blocks

This opens up many possibilities for quilt designs based on these kinds of shapes, such as Rail Fence, Square within a Square, Churn Dash, and so on. If you've dreamed of making a colorwash-type or garden quilt, but have dreaded piecing the tiny squares, here is your opportunity to make it with raw edges.

Other quilt patterns may also be used, but it can be tricky to get the raw edges to overlap correctly. Advance planning is required to cut the pieces the correct sizes so all the edges line up correctly. To avoid advance planning, cut the pieces to the finished size and butt the edges together. Baste carefully so the base fabric doesn't show through. Or use advance planning adding ¼" overlap to each side so the pieces overlap, resulting in the illusion of seamlines. The *Double Nine-Patch* on page 82 is a complex example of this. *Walkabout* on page 90 and *Through the Eyes of a Child* on page 91 and at right are simple examples, composed of all squares. This takes careful basting so the overlapped edges don't pull apart and make gaps.

TOP: Detail of a garden quilt, Walkabout, by Wendy Hill. Full quilt pictured on page 90.

BOTTOM: Detail of a garden quilt, Through the Eyes of a Child, by Debra Wruck. Full quilt pictured on page 91.

FABRIC ASSORTMENT AND QUANTITY

Make a scrappy surface with your scraps and leftovers, use your colorwash fabrics, or make repeat blocks with a unified color scheme. Remember, low contrast in color and value results in a blurring of the design when combined with surface stitching, while high-contrast fabrics remain more visible and distinct. Use the same fabric amounts as you would if the surface were being pieced.

CUTTING THE SHAPES

A rotary cutter, mat, and clear, gridded ruler make cutting the shapes accurate and easy. Handle the shapes with care to prevent fraying. If making a colorwashed-type quilt, sort the shapes by value. For repeat blocks, keep the shapes for each block together in a separate pile. Scrappy quilts can be sorted by the shape.

MARKING THE LAYOUT GRID

The quilt patterns discussed in this section are based on an underlying grid. The blocks fit into the grid; or the block can be divided into smaller grid units. When using raw-edge geometric shapes, an actual layout grid is created on a muslin or flannel base. Then the shapes are placed on the grid.

TOP: Low Contrast

BOTTOM: High Contrast

To make the layout grid, you'll need muslin or flannel fabric, a marking pen or pencil, and a clear, gridded ruler. Determine the size of the base, piecing the base fabric if necessary. Decide the size of the grid. For example, for a colorwash quilt design, the grid could be made up of 1½" squares. For a Rail Fence design, the grid might be 4" squares.

Draw a layout grid onto the quilter's flannel or muslin using a clear, gridded ruler and fabric marking pen or pencil. Square up two sides (one short, one long) before drawing the first line. Starting 1"–2" from the cut edge on the short side, draw the first line from one side to the other. Continue drawing lines the size of your grid until you come to the other side. Turn to the squared-up long side, start 1"–2" from the cut edge, and draw the first line, using the lines of the gridded ruler to keep this new line at right angles to the cross lines. Continue drawing lines the size of your grid until you come to the side. Extend the lines passed the grid as shown to allow for lining up the outer squares or blocks.

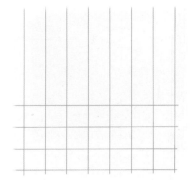

Layout grid

PLACEMENT OF THE SHAPES

Use a design wall or a large flat surface and fill in the grid with the pieces. When making a scrappy or colorwash-type surface, ignore details while laying out the pieces. Look instead for color and value placement until you get the layout you like. Repeat blocks may be filled in, arranged, and pinned in place as you go.

APPLYING THE BASIC STEPS

Refer to Chapter 1, page 17, to plan ahead for shrinkage and any special cutting layouts. When you collage geometric shapes for the surface, refer to Chapter 2, beginning on page 23, to determine the number of layers for your project. The shapes can be placed over a water soluble stabilizer, resulting in a very flexible, even fragile, surface-stitched piece. Placed over a fabric base, the piece can be drapey, but more substantial. When used with three layers (the shapes, a middle layer, and a lining), the piece can be firm to stiff. Determine the best method to secure the layers (Chapter 2, page 26). The shapes shift when handled during sewing, so take the time to secure the layers now for

more enjoyable sewing later. Chapter 6, beginning on page 57, gives you information about how to surface stitch.

TIP

When surface stitching through *all* the layers (rather than just the top layer), layer the gridded muslin onto the backing and sew through all the grid lines with water soluble basting thread or regular thread to match the backing, *before* laying out the geometric shapes.

DESIGN MOTIFS

A motif, defined as a distinctive figure in a design, can be found in printed fabric. Look for motifs to cut out in floral fabrics, animal or novelty prints, or other printed fabrics. Or make your own motifs using a template and any fabric.

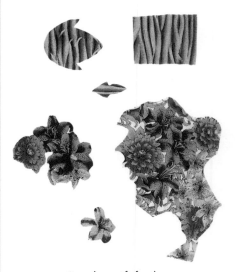

Sample motifs for the Fussy Cut Covered Pillow.

FABRIC ASSORTMENT

Look at fabric prints with an eye for seeing the individual motifs. When the motifs are separated from each other, just cut around the motif following the edge of the design. Sometimes the motifs are connected to each other; to cut out a single motif you may have to cut across another part of the design.

Any kind of washable fabric may be used. Iron flimsy fabric with spray starch to stiffen it and make it easier to handle. Avoid over-handling the cut motifs to prevent unwanted fraying. When using a lot of motifs, cut more than you anticipate actually using, so you can play with the placement.

You can also make your own motifs from print and solid fabrics. Use appliqué patterns, cookie cutter shapes, draw your own geometric or pictorial designs, or borrow motifs from copyright-free sources of design images. Cut the motifs from one piece of fabric, or build up the motif with cuttings from several fabrics.

PLACEMENT OF THE SHAPES

Motifs may be used alone to create the fabric surface, similar to using random shapes discussed earlier beginning on page 37. Just as with random shapes, the motifs may be scattered, clustered, or overlapped over a water soluble stabilizer for a very flexible piece, or over a base for a more firm result.

Use the raw-edge motifs as you would appliqué designs, without the hand or machine sewing. Arrange the motifs on the surface. The surface stitching holds them in place.

APPLYING THE BASIC STEPS

Refer to Chapter 1, page 17, to plan ahead for shrinkage and any special cutting layouts. When you collage design motifs for the surface, refer to Chapter 2, beginning on page 23, to determine the number of layers for your project. The shapes can be placed over a water soluble stabilizer, resulting in a very flexible, even fragile, surface stitched piece. Placed over a fabric base, the piece can be drapey, but more substantial. When used with three layers (the shapes, a middle layer, and a lining), the piece can be firm to stiff. Choose the best method to secure the layers and how to wash and dry your surface-stitched piece. Chapter 6, beginning on page 57, gives you information about how to surface stitch. After you have applied the three basic steps, continue as required to complete your project.

Applying the three basic steps for the Fussy Cut Covered Pillow

SPECIAL FEATURE:
MIX IT UP

Whole cloth and raw-edge collage can be used together. Try one of these ideas along with any of your own.

- Create a colorwash-type surface design on whole cloth with random shapes and cut motifs. Use large floral motifs for the foreground (bottom of the piece) and smaller motifs for the background (top of the piece). Experiment with something small, such as a vest or pillow top, or make the watercolor quilt wallhanging you've been dreaming about.

- Cut out folk or primitive looking shapes and arrange them over a plaid fabric base. Use cookie cutters, or just freehand cut stars, moons, hearts, trees, snowmen, cats, etc.

- Use any appliqué design with raw-edge shapes and surface stitching. Place the appliqué shapes over pieced blocks, borders of quilts, whole cloth, woven surfaces, raw-edge random shapes, print fabric, and more.

- Raw-edge collage "new" fabric to use as the underneath layer for a reverse appliqué bib and combine with surface-stitched whole cloth used for pockets and cuffs.

Folk or primitive shapes, detail of the Bamboo Shirt. Full garment pictured on page 114.

UPPER LEFT: Raw-edge random shapes and surface stitching over whole cloth base. Detail of Midnight Garden Wall Quilt. Full quilt pictured on page 96.

LOWER LEFT: By Wendy Hill, Overalls, Modeled by Cailin Sakaue (Blooming Baby Boutique, k.p. kids & co.)

UPPER RIGHT: Detail of Pocket

LOWER RIGHT: Detail of Cuffs

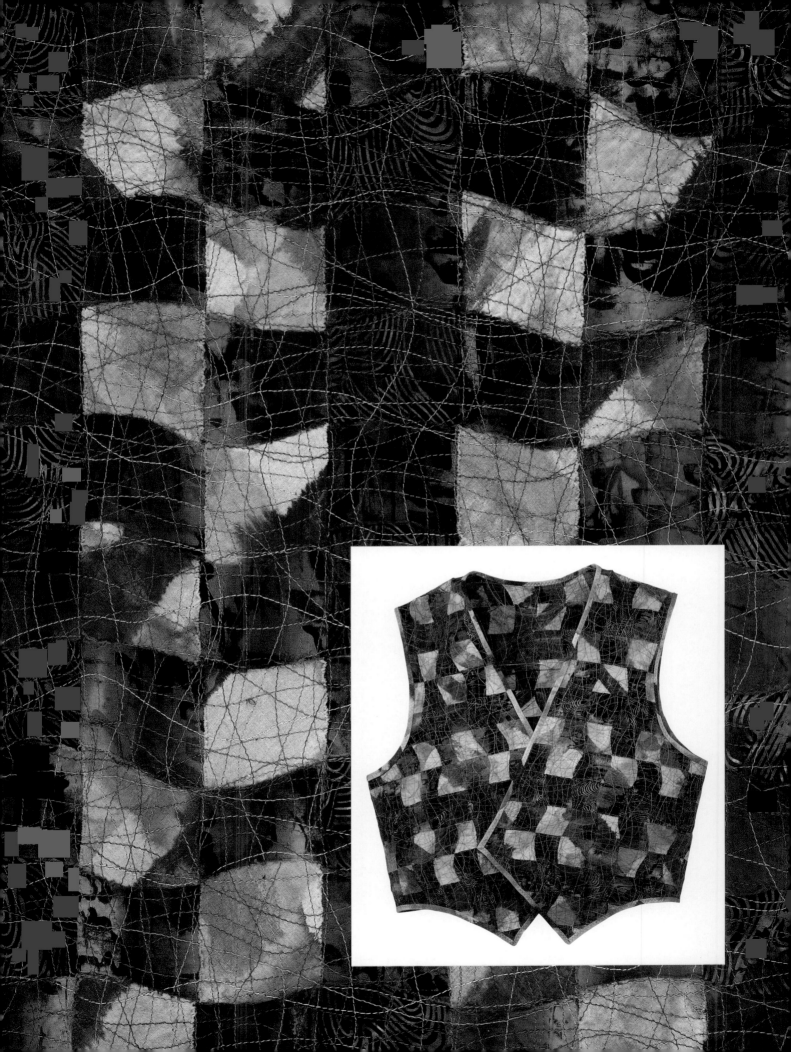

Chapter 5

WEAVING

INTRODUCTION

Weaving is found in most places and cultures around the world, and has been documented in some form as long as twenty thousand years ago. Technically, weaving is the interlacing of threads at right angles to form a web of fabric or cloth. The principle of weaving is the same no matter how simple or complex the weaving equipment or materials. Basically, in weaving there are stationary, vertical *warp* threads, crossed at right angles with horizontal, *weft* threads. The warp and weft interlock through the *over, under* motion of weaving, creating a new surface.

A SHORT COURSE IN OFF-LOOM WEAVING

The term "off-loom" refers to any method of weaving which does not require a frame, table, or floor loom to hold the warp stationary. While there are many kinds of off-loom weaving, a couple of methods using masking tape or pins have been adapted for use with fabric strips, ribbons, yarns, and other related fiber materials.

Become comfortable with the terms warp and weft. The warp is always the vertical threads or fabric strips. Generally, the warp is held firmly in place during the weaving process. The weft is always the horizontal threads or fabric strips. Also known as the filling, the weft is actively woven in and out of the warp to form the surface design.

All weaving patterns are derived from three basic patterns: plain, twill, and satin weaves. The plain weave, the most basic and commonly used in clothing and quilts, is the weaving pattern discussed in this book.

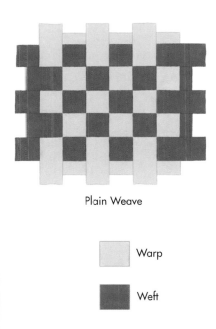

Plain Weave

☐ Warp

■ Weft

TEMPORARY LOOMS

For our purposes, off-loom techniques use masking tape and a flat surface, or pins and corrugated cardboard, to hold the warp material stationary. Use masking tape to hold the top and bottom ends of the warp material in place on a table top or other flat surface. (Warning: Masking tape can ruin the surface of your good dining room table.) This method is good for small and large projects, and is limited only by the size of the flat surface available to "string," or set up, the warp.

The use of pins and corrugated cardboard have come to be known as pin weaving. The pins are poked through the top and bottom ends of the warp material into the corrugated cardboard to hold the warp in place.

For traditional weaving, the warp and weft should cross each other at right angles. This alignment makes the most sturdy woven surface, a useful characteristic for making fabric which must be durable. It is a good idea to check the alignment during the weaving process, so corrections can be made along the way. Use a clear, gridded ruler to check the vertical and horizontal lines.

OVER, UNDER

The weft material is drawn over and under the warp. The plain weave is simply a row of "over, under, over, under" with a weft strip, alternated with a row of "under, over, under, over" with the following weft strip, repeated again and again. For weaving on a loom, a shuttle of some kind usually holds the weft material, unwinding it as it travels through the warp. In off-loom weaving with fabric strips and other fiber materials, the weft may be hand held and guided through the warp. Some people prefer to attach a safety pin to the end of a fabric strip or ribbon to have something to grip.

ASSEMBLING MATERIALS

Just about any material can be woven. For surface stitching, anything which meets the requirements of the end result will work. It must be washable, flexible, and you must be able to stitch through it. Just about any kind of fabric, many yarns, ribbons, narrow cording, rick-rack, lace trims, et cetera, can be used. Try wandering the aisles of your favorite craft store with an eye for new materials which may be incorporated into your next woven-surface project.

IDEAS FOR WEAVING

There are many ways to alter the look and effect of the plain weave with just a little knowledge, determination, and experimentation. Here are some ideas to get you started:

- Use one fabric for the warp and a different fabric for the weft. This makes a checkerboard pattern.

Checkerboard

- Use an assortment of fabrics in the warp and weft. For a scrappy look, position the strips randomly. For a pattern, repeat the colors in the warp, in the weft.

- Use the same width of strips in the warp and weft to make a pattern of squares. Unequal-width strips make a pattern of rectangles. Strips cut with wavy or irregular angles make a pattern of odd shapes when woven.

Rectangles

Odd Shapes

- Try the basket weave variation of a plain weave. Instead of "over, under," the basket weave is based on "over, over, under, under" and the alternate "under, under, over, over" for the next row.

Basket Weave

- Leave a gap of space between the warp and weft strips when weaving. When layered over another fabric, the background fabric shows through the holes. If layered over water soluble stabilizer, the open areas will be filled up with just thread from the surface stitching for an unusual effect.

Plain weave with gaps between warp and weft strips

- Mix up the materials in the warp and weft, using fabric, ribbon, cording, and so on.

- Sew different fabric strips together end to end to create color changes in the warp and weft. Or overlap the two ends in an "under" spot on the back side of the weaving.

- The warp and weft do not have to be kept at right angles when surface stitching the surface. This opens up a whole new avenue for exploration, which you may want to try after gaining experience using traditional weaves.

For more ideas about variations of the plain weave, look for books of basic weaving patterns. Almost any of these may be adapted to use with fabric and other materials.

TIP

Before you start cutting into your fabric, try experimenting with magazine photographs. Cut the photographs with an old rotary cutter blade, weave a practice design over a surface of fusible interfacing, and fuse according to manufacturer's instructions. Make notes on the back for future reference.

WEAVING METHODS

Here are three specific methods for using weaving with surface stitching: raw-edge weaving with a whole-cloth base; weaving with tubes, bias, and raw-edge strips; and pin weaving. Along with the general information about weaving, this chapter will provide you with what you need to know to use a variety of weaving methods with surface stitching for clothing, quilts, and other great stuff.

RAW-EDGE WEAVING WITH A WHOLE-CLOTH WARP BASE

This is an easy way to get started. The *warp* is cut from one piece of fabric. The *weft* strips are cut from one or more different fabrics. Small projects are easier to handle, but the only real size restriction is the size of the flat surface under the weaving. Tightly woven fabrics with a high thread count are easier to use because they don't ravel as much as more loosely woven fabrics, but any fabric can be used if your heart is set on it.

CUTTING

Use scissors or a rotary cutter, mat, and ruler. To cut the warp strips, start at the bottom of the whole cloth and cut to within ½" of the other side, leaving the top edge intact. Cut freehand wavy or irregular strips, or measure with the gridded ruler to cut even or uneven straight strips. Move the cutting mat as needed when using a rotary cutter. Continue until the whole piece has been cut into strips.

Top edge intact

Freehand wavy or angular strips

Measured strips

Cut the weft strips next. The weft fabrics may also be cut with straight, wavy, or angular lines, same or different widths, and measured or freehand.

WEAVING ON A TEMPORARY LOOM

Before beginning a project using raw-edge weaving with a whole cloth base, review the next section, "Applying the Basic Steps," to determine the number of layers needed.

Beginning with an optional water soluble and/or fabric base (secured with masking tape), place the cut whole-cloth warp fabric right side up on a flat surface large enough to accommodate the entire piece of fabric. This is where the actual weaving will take place, so pick a place your project can "live" until woven. Use masking tape to secure the top uncut edge of the whole-cloth warp fabric. Straighten the warp strips so they lie flat next to each other. Tape the bottom of the warp strips if desired, or leave them loose.

Start weaving at the top, snuggling the first weft strip up against the intact edge. Before continuing, check to make sure the weft is at right angles to the warp.

Continue to add weft strips, juggling each strip into position, until finished. Make any needed adjustments to ensure the warp and weft are at right angles, then read the next section for how to proceed.

APPLYING THE BASIC STEPS

Refer to Chapter 1, page 17, to plan ahead for shrinkage and any special cutting layouts. When weaving to create the surface, refer to Chapter 2, beginning on page 23, to determine the number of layers for your project. Weaving over water soluble stabilizer results in a very flexible, even fragile (depending on the materials) surface-stitched piece. Placed over a fabric base (which will be three layers altogether), the piece can be drapey to firm. Adding a fourth layer (woven top, middle layer, and fabric base) will result in a firm to stiff surface-stitched piece. Determine the best method to secure the layers (Chapter 2, page 26). Unless the piece is very small, the weight of the woven piece will pull itself

apart with handling, so avoid heartbreak by taking the time to do it right. Try hand basting each warp and weft strip with water soluble thread. If using a stabilizer or base fabric, pin basting will hold everything together. Pin through the layers with enough pins to be able to maneuver the piece through the sewing machine. Chapter 6, beginning on page 57, gives you information about how to surface stitch. Wash and dry your surface-stitched piece (Chapter 2, page 29). After you have applied the three basic steps, continue as required to complete your project.

WEAVING WITH TUBES, BIAS, AND RAW-EDGE STRIPS

The previous section described weaving using one fabric for the warp. In this section weaving with three different types of individual warp and weft strips will be discussed: make tubes of fabric and press them flat; use a bias maker to make bias strips (bias makers come in a variety of sizes); or cut strips with straight, wavy, or angular sides and leave the edges raw.

The weaving process is the same. Follow "A Short Course in Off-Loom Weaving," beginning on page 47. Weave on a flat surface over any water soluble stabilizer or base fabrics. Use masking tape to attach the top of the warp strips to the surface; tape the bottom of the strips if desired. Weave the weft strips, checking for proper alignment, and snuggling each strip next to the one above.

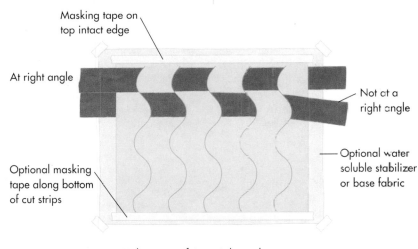

Masking tape on top intact edge

At right angle

Optional masking tape along bottom of cut strips

Not at a right angle

Optional water soluble stabilizer or base fabric

Make sure weft is at right angles to warp.

TUBES

Cut the fabric strips on the straight of the grain unless a bias cut would take advantage of a plaid, stripe, or other print. To calculate how wide to cut the strip, multiply two times the finished width of the tube and add the seam allowance. For example, the strips for a 2" tube need to be cut 4½" (2" x 2" = 4", plus ½" for two ¼" seam allowances). A fabric tube is made by sewing a strip wrong sides together, then pressing the seam flat, with the seam down the middle of the back of the tube.

Tube for non-reversible weaving

For reversible tube weaving, sew the tubes right sides together, turn, then press flat with the seam down the side, so the seam will be hidden.

Tube for reversible weaving

Any fabric can be used without regard to fraying, and tubes give a more finished look. On the down side, tubes require a lot of fabric, and they are heavier than bias or raw-edge strips when made from the same fabric.

BIAS STRIPS

Called "bias" strips, these can be made starting with strips cut on a true bias or the straight of the grain. Save time by making bias strips with a gadget called a bias strip maker, following the manufacturer's instructions. It is possible to hand fold the edges of the strip to the center of the back, but this is very time consuming

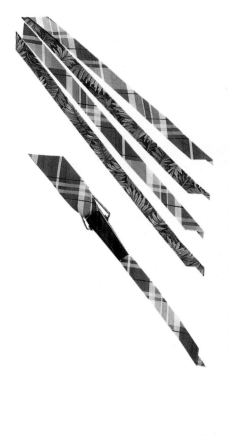

and difficult to do accurately. Look for ready-made bias strips in the notions department of fabric or craft stores; some stores carry decorator fabric bias strips in addition to the solid colors.

Any fabric can be used, but some fabrics hold a crease better than others. Avoid the frustration of finding your freshly made bias strips popped open by winding the strips onto a piece of cardboard or around a small box. Bias strips look more finished than raw-edge strips, without the weight of a tube. When using a bias maker you will be limited to a small number of available sizes, and must purchase each size bias maker separately.

Bias Strips

RAW-EDGE STRIPS

There are two advantages of raw-edge strips; one is the freedom of cutting the strips straight, wavy, or irregularly; the other is the ability to weave anything from light to stiff, by adding more layers. If you like the look of raw edges, this is the way to go.

Strips cut with straight edges from an assortment of fabrics will naturally fit together side by side. This is not so with wavy or irregularly-cut strips, unless the strips are all cut from one piece of fabric and woven in the order they were cut, or are cut in a special way. To use different fabrics, try this trick: Overlap two fabrics along the shared edge, then cut through both layers at the same time; throw away the excess; continue with the next fabric. When you are ready, weave these strips in order so they are placed side by side in the warp or weft.

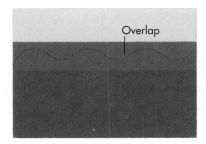

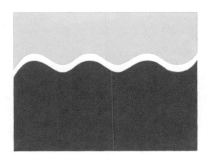

Cutting adjacent wavy strips

APPLYING THE BASIC STEPS

Refer to Chapter 1, page 17, to plan ahead for shrinkage and any special cutting layouts. When weaving to create the surface, refer to Chapter 2, beginning on page 23, to determine the number of layers for your project and the best method to secure the layers. Unless the piece is very small, the weight of the woven piece will pull itself apart with handling. Try hand basting each warp and weft strip with water soluble thread. If using a stabilizer or base fabric, pin basting will hold everything together. Pin through the layers with enough pins to be able to maneuver the piece through the sewing machine. Chapter 6, beginning on page 57, gives you information about how to surface stitch. Wash and dry your surface stitched piece (Chapter 2, page 29). After you have applied the three basic steps, continue as required to complete your project.

PIN WEAVING

Combine pin weaving with surface stitching for an interesting mix of textures and crinkle. Pin weaving gets its name from the kind of off-loom weaving method used: corrugated cardboard and pins. Commonly associated with making vests using ribbons and yarn in the warp, and bias strips of fabric in the weft, this method can be used with any combination of materials.

A mix of ribbons, rick-rack, and bias strips on pin-woven appliqué heart for child's sundress by Wendy Hill. Full garment pictured on page 113.

ASSEMBLING MATERIALS

You'll need a piece of corrugated cardboard large enough to accommodate the woven surface. For stability, pin weave directly over a water soluble stabilizer, or for more weight, over muslin or fashion fabric. Purchased or drawn grid paper is strongly recommended, especially for beginners; use a one-half- or one-inch grid. You will also need long quilter's pins, masking tape, and a wide assortment of ribbons, rickrack, fabric strips (bias, tubes, or raw edge), and so on.

GETTING STARTED

Start with the cardboard on the bottom. Tape the optional grid paper in place on the cardboard.

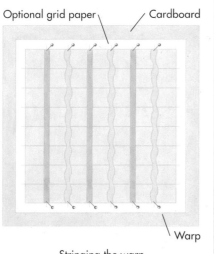

Optional grid paper   Cardboard

Warp

Stringing the warp

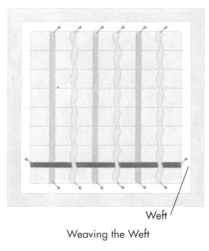

Weft

Weaving the Weft

Place the stabilizer or fabric on top and tape in place. If using water soluble stabilizer, you'll be able to see the grid lines through the see-through material. When using a fabric base, make sure the grid lines extend beyond the edge of the fabric so you can see them.

PREPARING THE WARP

Measure the length of the warp from the top of the surface to be woven to the bottom. Cut the warp materials this length plus 1". Attach the warp materials over the grid lines and secure in place with pins along the top and bottom edges of the warp, stretching the warp material a little bit to make it slightly taut. Do not overstretch. This is called "stringing" the warp. Continue until the entire weaving surface has been "strung."

WEAVING

Weave the weft materials through the warp. Check to make sure the warp and weft form right angles, unless you want to skew the warp and weft on purpose. When weaving with yarns, ribbons, and other soft, pliable materials, you have the option of tightly packing the weft material together, almost covering up the warp, or positioning the weft material more loosely.

APPLYING THE BASIC STEPS

Refer to Chapter 1, page 17, to plan ahead for shrinkage and any special cutting layouts. When weaving to create the surface, refer to Chapter 2, beginning on page 23, to determine the number of layers for your project and the best method to secure the layers. A pin woven surface is very fragile until it is secured in place. The best way is to sandwich the entire pin-woven surface with a piece of water soluble stabilizer. Pin through the layers with enough pins to be able to maneuver the piece through the sewing machine. Chapter 6, beginning on page 57, gives you information about how to surface stitch. Wash and dry your surface-stitched piece (Chapter 2, page 29). After you have applied the three basic steps, continue as required to complete your project.

SPECIAL FEATURE: MIX IT UP

Woven surfaces may be used by themselves, or in combination with whole cloth and raw-edge collage. A whole new world of opportunity is waiting for you. Try these ideas or some of your own combinations.

- Start with a whole-cloth surface. Weave only small sections of the surface. Cut the small sections into strips and weave with strips the same or different width. These may be sandwiched with water soluble stabilizer, basted with water soluble thread, or pin basted.

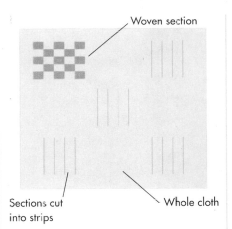

Woven section

Sections cut into strips

Whole cloth

Weave sections of a whole-cloth surface.

- Weave a fabric surface. Cut raw-edge shapes from a solid, print, plaid, or another woven surface and arrange them over the woven surface for added contrast.

- Weave two fabric surfaces. Cut both into strips and weave together. For the most contrast, use highly contrasting fabrics or surfaces woven from different sized strips.

- Piece or appliqué a fabric surface, cut it into warp strips, leaving the top edge intact (page 49), and weave through it. An illusion is formed in which the eye alternately sees a checker-board or the complete picture of the pieced or appliquéd surface.

Raw-edge shapes arranged over a woven surface

Weaving an Illusion

Chapter 6
SURFACE STITCHING

THREAD MEDLEYS

As discussed in Chapter 1, page 9, thread of any fiber content and in sizes ranging from 30 to 80 may be used. Now it is time to select the thread colors to go with your fabrics. Try the following strategy or your own method for gathering together a great group of threads.

Look for the predominant colors found in your selected fabrics, and with great spirit and wild abandon, begin picking out these colors in thread. Pay attention to the small amounts of accent colors in the fabric, and add these thread colors to the collection.

After accumulating a variety, sort the thread into piles according to color families. For example, cluster all the reds into one pile, all the purples into another pile, and so on. Organize the spools of thread in each pile from light to dark. Playing with the spools this way will spark new ways of looking at the thread and fabric colors. A new family of colors may emerge, and if it does, cluster these spools into

their own pile. For example, a family of red-violets may come out of the two groups of red and purple threads.

Next, look for thread colors which could form a link between the piles of color families. This link is a kind of cross between two colors. For example, link a pile of blues and a pile of greens with a light or dark blue-green. Often the thread

colors linked between color families will turn out to be surprising accents. Try anything at this experimental stage.

It's hard to resist adding just one more spool of thread, yet only so much thread can be layered on any given fabric surface. Stop adding thread, and push the linked thread colors into a color family pile.

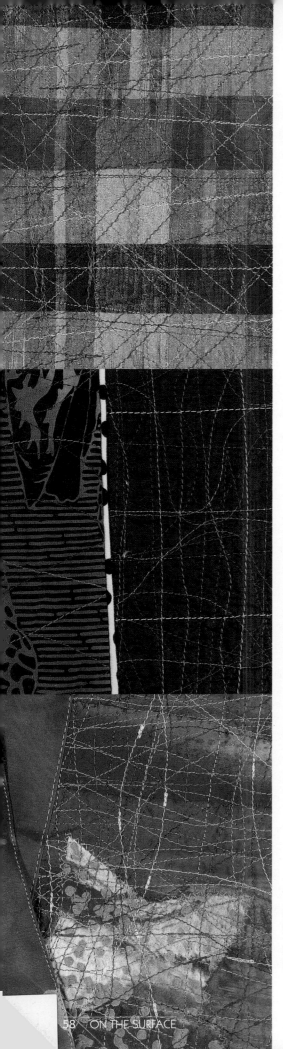

Using the number of spools required for a similar project in Chapter 7 as a guide, start the narrowing down and selection process. Take one spool of thread from each pile until you have a good distribution of lights and darks that total the number of spools you need. Store each chosen color family of thread in a separate bag. (When selecting spools of thread at your local retailer, offer to return unwanted thread to the display case.)

THREAD ORDER

Surface stitching may appear to be a random but uniform layering of thread over the surface, but there is some method behind all the stitching madness. The primary quality to achieve with classic Wendy Hill surface stitching is an even density and distribution of color and texture. It is difficult to be truly random on purpose without some kind of organized plan. First, plan the order in which you'll use the thread.

Sort the threads into three piles: those that blend with the fabrics; those that offer medium contrast with the fabrics; and those that create the most contrast.

One strategy is to use an even mix of contrasting threads right from the start. Instead of sorting by contrast, group the threads by the color families. This means there will be lights and darks in each pile. Alternating piles, take a thread from each pile and add a layer of stitching. The result is an even blend of colors with high texture (top photo).

Another strategy is to start stitching with the group of least contrasting threads first, followed by the medium-contrast threads, and finally the high-contrast threads. This results in high texture with mostly the final few layers of threads really showing off (center photo).

A third strategy is to reverse this order by starting with the most contrasting threads and ending with the lowest contrast threads for another strategy. The difference is subtle, but the result will be high texture and more colors showing through the mix (bottom photo).

In a very real sense it doesn't matter which way you choose to use the thread colors. The important factor is having a specific plan so the thread colors are truly distributed evenly across the surface.

TOP: Even mix of contrasting threads.

CENTER: Stitched with least contrasting threads first.

BOTTOM: Stitched with most contrasting threads first.

STITCH STYLES

The first spool is threaded on the sewing machine and ready to go, but how do you start stitching? It is helpful to plan how to stitch, using one of the six basic stitch styles: pivot, crosshatch, wavy, circular, under or over grid, and inspirational. All six are based on a straight stitch, with a regular (or walking) presser foot and the feed dogs up on the sewing machine. You can use one stitch style throughout, or a combination of styles, as the layers of thread are added over the fabric surface.

Surface stitching a large area, such as a quilt, is easier if the sides are rolled to eliminate the bulk and weight that will pull on the needle. Instead of trying to stitch from one side of a large surface to another, stitch small adjacent areas, working around the piece until the surface is covered with each thread color. Stitch right up to the edges. If you become discouraged, remember, things worth doing are often time consuming; you will be rewarded for your effort.

PIVOT

For sewing machines with reverse capability, simply stitch forward, then in reverse, pivoting at the point in which the direction is changed. Ideally, the reverse stitch heads back at a slightly different angle so the stitching is not on top of itself. With practice, the fabric may be tugged a little to make the pivot without stopping the machine and lifting the presser foot.

For forward-stitching-only machines, stop the machine at the desired pivot point (needle down), lift up the presser foot, and turn the fabric around. Put down the presser foot and straight stitch to the next pivot point; then, repeat the process.

The stitching lines may be straight or wavy between pivot points.

Short stretches of stitching between points results in more dense coverage of thread, while long sweeping lengths of stitching separate the pivot points for less dense coverage.

Straight Pivot

Wavy Pivot

Short stitching lines

Long, sweeping stitching lines

Unstitched   First Layers of Pivot Points   Multiple Layers of Pivot Points

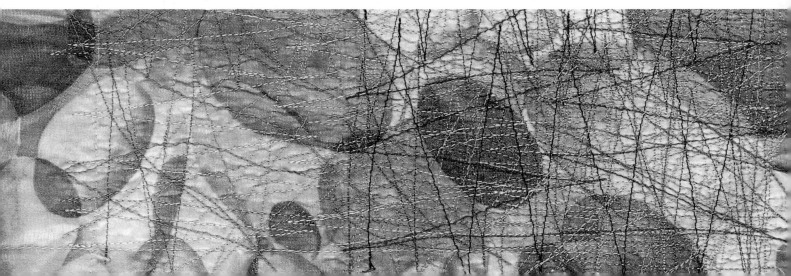

When a row of pivot points is completed, drop down and pivot stitch your way back to the other side, adding another row of pivot points.

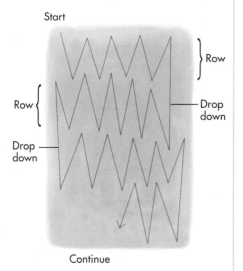

Avoid creating sharp lines along the rows of pivot points by overlapping the pivot points as each successive row is added.

Overlap pivot points between rows

Pivot stitch styles tend to use more thread, and are more time consuming than other stitch styles. However, more density and texture are added with this stitch style. The pivot stitch style is more visible than other styles, especially when a high-contrast thread color or thick thread is used.

CROSSHATCH

The idea behind crosshatch stitching is to have vertical and horizontal (or diagonal) parallel lines intersecting each other. The parallel lines are only roughly parallel—no measuring, please.

Vertical/horizontal Crosshatch

Diagonal Crosshatch

One way to crosshatch stitch is to start and stop with each row of stitching. This can be tedious, with all the raising and lowering of the presser foot and snipping

thread ends. The other way is to stitch across to the other side of the fabric, pivot and stitch along the edge for a short distance, then pivot again and stitch back across to the other side. This allows a continuous stitching line.

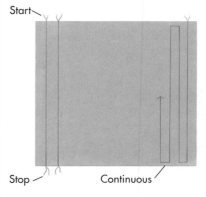

The stitched lines can be kept very straight, or may be wavy or slightly irregular. Crosshatching uses less thread than pivot stitching. Also, it is easier to control the density because there is no bunching of thread in any one area as with the pivot points. This is a good "filler" stitch to use with other stitch styles to fill in bare spots.

Unstitched   First Layers of Crosshatching   Multiple Layers of Crosshatching

WAVY

Stitching wavy lines involves a motion similar to holding the steering wheel while driving a car. With the hands at about ten o'clock and two o'clock on the fabric surface, make a slight back and forth motion; this causes the line to be wavy. Wavy lines may go across the fabric in any direction: crossing themselves any which way or keeping the curves of the wavy lines separated.

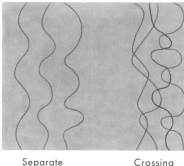

Separate
Wavy Lines

Crossing
Wavy Lines

Vary the depth of the wavy lines, creating shallow or deep curves as you stitch. To help visualize the curves, imagine gliding down a powdery slope, "skiing" across the fabric, leaving curved tracks in the snow.

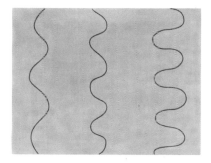

Different depths of curved stitching lines

Almost anything goes with wavy stitching lines, so the best way to create uniform density is to stitch repetitiously in a particular manner across the entire surface. Then choose another direction and style of wavy lines in which to cross the surface, changing thread colors as you go.

CIRCULAR

It is actually possible to turn the fabric surface around and around with the feed dogs up using a regular or walking presser foot. The only genuine limiting factor is the size of the fabric surface; large pieces are difficult to squeeze through the space between the needle and the machine. With this stitch style, keep turning the fabric in one direction, or stitch circles to the right for awhile, then reverse directions and stitch circles to the left. The circles may be as large or small as you can manage on your fabric surface.

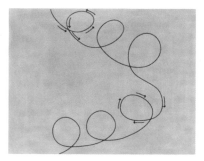

Circular stitching to right and left

Wavy Lines

Circular Lines

Compared with other stitch styles, it is harder to control direction and density with just circular stitching. It takes some practice to keep turning the fabric while stitching, so start with a slow speed. Remember, it is only the small area around the presser foot which must be flat; it doesn't matter how the rest of the fabric surface is bunched or scrunched. This stitch style is easier to use after the surface has been textured with other stitching. The circular lines, whether used alone or in combination with other stitching, add a fun, loopy texture that is worth the extra effort.

UNDER OR OVER GRID

This is a supplementary stitch style to be used with other stitch styles. The primary effect of this stitch style is to add a unifying force of pattern and color over the surface, either under all the other surface stitching, or on top. Although called a grid, this also includes parallel lines.

Parallel Lines

Perpendicular Lines

The scale of the grid or parallel lines may be anywhere from ½" to several inches apart, depending on the size of the finished piece. It really is not necessary to measure these lines; slight irregularities are part of the surface-stitched look.

Unstitched   Perpendicular Lines

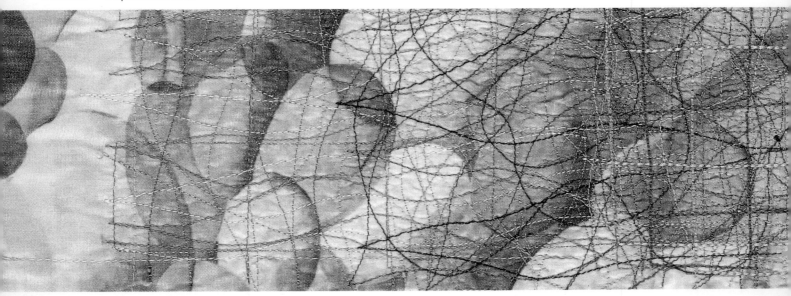

There are several ways to make the under or over grid stand out from the rest of the stitching. Choose a bright, contrasting color or a flashy, shiny specialty thread. Topstitching or thicker embroidery threads stand out because of the contrast in thickness of the thread. Use two threads through one needle, or a variegated thread to make the stitch lines prominent. A kind of "plaid" can be made by using a medley of colors in the grid.

When stitched first, the under grid is more subtle, blurred somewhat by the layers of stitching over it. When stitched last, the over grid seems to pull together the random stitching beneath it. This stitch is not meant to add texture; it's a good way to sparingly use the more expensive specialty threads, as it generally requires small amounts of thread.

IMPROVISATIONAL

This is a mix of some or all of the above, with a little whimsy and abandon thrown in for good measure. A good time to become improvisational is after a good texture has been established through several layers of stitching. Whether you just don't care any more near the end of the surface stitching, or you need to zip around to fill in bare spots, the improvisational method is both fun and practical.

UPPER: Parallel Lines

LOWER: Improvisational

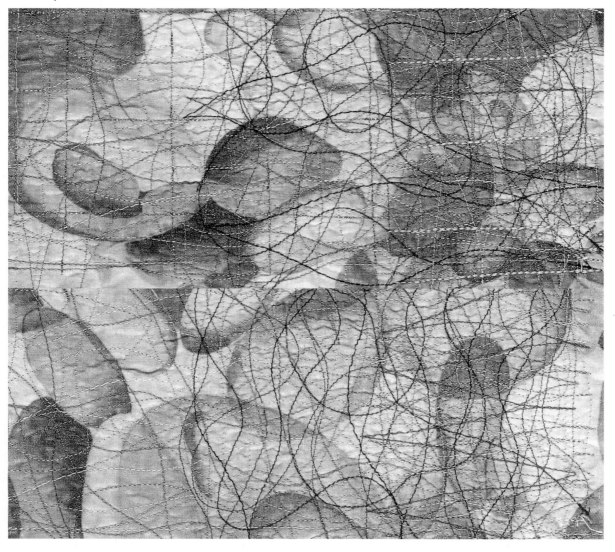

VARIATIONS ON A STRAIGHT STITCH

One of the primary claims of classic Wendy Hill surface stitching is the use of the straight stitch—nothing but the straight stitch. Surely at one time a straight stitch was nothing but a straight stitch; but today variations of the straight stitch exist, and these must be discussed for this section to be complete.

▌ The stitch length may be adjusted from very short to very long. Short and long stitch lengths look different, so this is an easy way to change the look of your surface stitching.

▌ For another easy modification, vary the thickness of the thread used. Thicker thread makes a thicker line, while thinner thread makes a thinner line. Again, thick and thin lines alter the look of the surface-stitched fabric. Another way to get the look of a thick thread is to run two threads through one needle. Use highly contrasting thread colors to get the most out of this trick.

▌ Variegated thread changes colors along the length of the thread, repeating the color pattern over and over. This is a good way to make the surface stitching look more complex and colorful with just one sweep across the surface.

▌ Investigate the special stitch capabilities of your sewing machine, especially under the heading of "utility stitching," avoiding any recognizable embroidery stitches. Under the names of "saddle," "double," and "triple" stitches, the sewing machine sews forward and backward in some combination to make a thick, strong, and flexible straight stitch. Intended to make a strong seam, use it for surface stitching when a strong-looking line is needed.

▌ Another variation of a straight stitch is called a "stretch" stitch, generally used for sewing knits and bias seams. This stitch is ever so slightly jagged, looking like tiny lightning bolts for interesting added texture.

▌ A stitch used for outlining designs alternates stitching in place with stitching forward, a useful variation for adding "blips" of texture along the line of straight stitching. If your machine doesn't have this stitch setting, it can be duplicated manually. Affectionately called the "ee-ee" stitch, create it by sewing forward, then at intervals using the reverse control, in a few short bursts, to stitch back and forth on the same spot. (Say "ee—ee—ee—ee" as you go back and forth.) When used in concentration with a few different colors of threads, these little "blips" add a very textured and almost tweedy look.

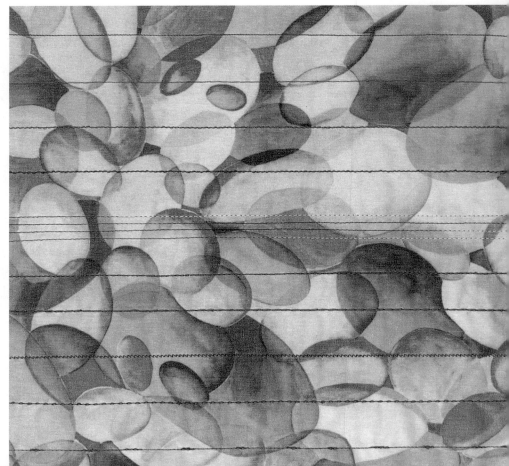

Variation of a Straight Stitch

With experience, and specific knowledge of your sewing machine, you'll discover other variations of the straight stitch. Use any of these altered straight stitches with any of the stitch styles for an infinite combination of looks with your surface stitching. A cautionary reminder—basic straight-stitch surface stitching looks every bit as good as stitching with a large variety of straight stitches, so don't feel pressured to explore further until you are ready to do so.

TIP
Surface stitching is easy, but it takes time. Try listening to a book on tape or the radio while stitching.

SURFACE STITCHING GUIDELINES

■ Don't make stitched lines of any one thread color too close together. It is the accumulation of multiple layers of thread which results in a densely covered fabric surface.

■ Avoid stitching on the same lines over and over. As you stitch, aim toward areas with less stitching, gradually filling in the bare spots.

■ When stitching over a surface with raw edges, stitch along the raw edges when the opportunity arises. All the raw edges will not be stitched by any one thread color, but with the accumulation of layers of thread, most of the raw edges can be caught by one color or another.

■ Trim the thread ends as you go, especially with reversible pieces. Loose thread ends get caught up in the layers of stitching, making them just about impossible to pick out later.

■ Judge how far a particular color needs to be distributed before starting. For uniformity, each color should be evenly spread out over all the fabric to be surface stitched. For example, if you have one small spool of pink to spread over three vest pieces, use a stitch style with widely separated lines of stitching.

■ It is actually possible to have so much surface stitching that the fabric is no longer visible, and the thread layers look cloudy. Even densely stitched fabric has spaces at least ⅜" square between lines of thread, with many spaces larger than this.

■ Always surface stitch right up to the edges of the fabric surface. After washing and shrinking, you may need every inch of fabric, so it should be uniform. Also, areas with less thread will shrink differently; for uniform shrinking, start with uniform stitching.

■ If unsure when enough is enough, throw the surface-stitched piece into the washer and dryer. Sparse areas and bald spots show up as obvious areas of little or no crinkle. If necessary, press the piece flat, add more stitching where needed, and repeat the trip through the washer and dryer until you are satisfied with the result.

TIP
Surface stitching can look unappealing during the first few layers of thread. Don't get discouraged. Keep stitching.

SUMMARY

Our love of fabric is closely connected to the appeal of both visual and physical texture. Surface stitching and fabric manipulation is all about creating texture in our quilts, clothing, and more. The best news is that this technique may be used by everyone, from beginner to experienced sewer. Continue to Chapter 7 and discover the joys of surface stitching for yourself. Some of the items presented in Chapter 7 are *projects* with supply lists and instructions and some are *inspirational starting points* that include information about how the item was created. You can use these as starting points to create your own original piece.

Chapter 7
PROJECTS
AND INSPIRATIONAL STARTING POINTS

INTRODUCTION

Surface stitching, the layering of stitches over a fabric surface, can be applied to anything which can be made of fabric. Keep it simple by using purchased fabric, or manipulate the fabric surface first with piecing, appliqué, raw-edge collage, weaving, or all of the above. This is an open-ended technique—the applications of surface stitching and fabric manipulation are as diverse as the people who use them. The ideas are endless.

The different results of surface stitching and fabric manipulation all have the basic steps in common. Turn the following pages and open the doors to the possibilities with quilts, clothing, things for the home, and small projects. The basics provided in the first six chapters will give you the confidence needed to start your own surface stitched project.

Ten of the following samples are given as projects, with supply lists and complete step-by-step instructions. All fabric measurements are based on fabric 44"-45" wide unless otherwise stated. The remaining approximately thirty samples are given as inspirational starting points. Enough information is provided for you to apply it with your own ideas and patterns.

For continuity, the projects and inspirational samples are grouped by quilts, clothing, things for the home and small projects. By all means, save all your leftovers, no matter how small. Leftovers can be used for making jewelry, greeting cards, light switch plate covers, collaged wallhangings, and much more.

QUILTS

Quilts and surface-stitched texture go naturally together. This section includes both bed and wall quilts, with something for everybody. Surface stitch an antique looking coverlet, a folky lap quilt, a contemporary Log Cabin twin bed quilt, or one of many collaged, pieced, or appliquéd wall quilts. Or finish a quilt top you already have. The only real limit to the possibilities open to you is the time to make all the projects you have ideas for.

TRIANGLE BABY QUILT

PROJECT

Method: whole cloth (pieced), surface stitching through the three layers

Stitch Style: straight and wavy pivots; wavy lines

I designed this quilt to use up leftover half-square triangles from another baby quilt project. It is made of 80 pieced 3" squares; each square is made of 2 half-square triangles (160 triangles total). Setting the blocks on point with muslin squares set off the scrappy looking pieced blocks and made the quilt larger. The neutral background also showcases the surface stitching by Debra Wruck, who also pieced the quilt. This quilt uses the whole cloth variation of piecing a whole surface first, with surface stitching through all the layers. You can use a quilt top you already have and follow Steps 13–18 to finish it using your own measurements.

I used 3" half-square triangle paper to make the squares with an assortment of about twenty different fabrics in color-saturated and deep pastel colors. Using the 6" finished blocks, Debra pieced the top, stacked the layers with quilter's flannel in the middle, and basted with water soluble thread. She surface stitched through all the layers with about thirty assorted pastel threads, ranging from pale to bright colors. After washing and drying, Debra squared up the quilt and added the double French fold binding cut from a multicolored print.

SUPPLIES

multicolored print/theme fabric: ⅜ yard

solid-appearing prints: ⅛ yard each of approximately 19 fabrics

white muslin or cotton fabric for alternate squares and outer border: 2½ yards

backing: 1¾ yards of 60"-wide or 3 yards of 44"-wide

quilter's flannel for middle layer: 3 yards

solid-appearing print for inner border: ¾ yard

fabric for double French fold binding: ¾ yard

thread: 30 assorted spools

water soluble basting thread

3" half-square triangle paper (optional)

Triangle Baby Quilt, 49½" x 58",
Debra Wruck and Wendy Hill

As with all surface-stitched fabric, shrinkage occurs in the washing and drying step, as well as during the surface stitching process. The dimensions given during the assembly process are before shrinking. The amount of shrinkage varies a little with the fabrics, threads, and amount of stitching used. It is not necessary to prewash fabrics, as they will shrink anyway, unless you want to check the fabric colors to be sure they will not run or bleed in the wash.

STEP 1

Familiarize yourself with the quilt design by referring to the photograph.

Four squares are sewn together to make A blocks and B blocks. A blocks do not contain any theme fabric, and each triangle is a different print fabric. B blocks have four theme fabric triangles and four different prints. There are 10 each of the A and B blocks.

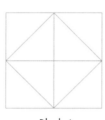

Block A

Block B

STEP 2

Method 1

For quick assembly, use 3" half-square triangle paper to make the pieced squares (according to the manufacturer's directions). You will need:

40 squares with one theme fabric and one print

40 squares with two different prints (pair up different combinations of your prints)

OR

Method 2

Use your favorite rotary or template method to achieve 3" finished half-square triangles. You will need:

40 theme fabric triangles

120 assorted print fabric triangles

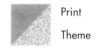

Print
Theme

Print
Print

STEP 3

Arrange the squares to make 10 A blocks. On a large flat surface or design wall, put four squares together to form a "square within a square," making sure no two identical prints are in one block.

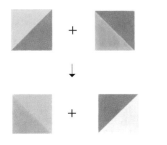

STEP 4

Arrange the remaining squares to make 10 B blocks. On a large flat surface or design wall, put four squares together so the theme fabric forms a "square within a square" with no two identical prints in the same block.

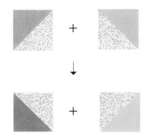

STEP 5

Fiddle with the placement until you are satisfied. Then sew the squares to make the blocks. First place right sides together of two squares and join with a ¼" seam allowance. Press the seams open. Then place the two half-squares right sides together and stitch. Press the seams open. Repeat with the remaining 19 blocks (both A and B).

STEP 6

Cut white alternate squares, half-square and quarter-square setting triangles. You will need:

12 alternate blocks, each 6½" square

14 half-square setting triangles (seven 6⅞" squares, cut in half diagonally)

4 quarter-square setting triangles (one 7¼" square, cut in quarters diagonally)

STEP 7

Lay out the pieced and alternate blocks on a large flat surface or design wall. Follow the photograph. Arrange the blocks until you like the placement; but remember, this is a scrappy quilt, and almost any arrangement will be great.

STEP 8

Stitch the blocks together in diagonal rows with triangles at each end. Press. Then stitch the rows together. Add remaining two corner triangles. Press the seams open. Square up the inner quilt top.

STEP 9

Cut four 3½" strips across the width of the fabric for the inner print border.

STEP 10

Starting with the longer sides of the inner quilt, pin and stitch the inner border strips with right sides together. Square up the corner, trimming off the excess fabric. Press the seams open. Repeat with the remaining sides. Press the seams open. Square up the corners, trimming off the excess fabric.

STEP 11

Cut eight 7" strips across the width of the fabric for the outer border. Stitch two of the strips together along a short end with right sides together; press the seams open. Repeat three more times. You will have a total of four strips. This allows you to place the seams where desired when attaching the borders.

WHITE-ON-WHITE COVERLET

PROJECT

Method: whole cloth, surface stitching through three layers

Stitch Style: straight and wavy pivots

If you love the look and feel of an old-timey quilt, you'll love this project, designed and made by me.

This coverlet was designed for a twin bed. To make a larger coverlet, piece fabrics together to make the size desired. As with machine quilting, you'll want to roll up the sides of the coverlet when stitching to make it easier to handle. Full instructions for the coverlet follow, with templates for the scalloped edges.

Making the bed at The Peacock Inn, Grass Valley, California, White-on-White Coverlet, 40" x 63", Wendy Hill; White-on-White Pillowcases and Pillow (with button closure), Wendy Hill, Kelly Simbirdi, Sandy Radtke

SUPPLIES

white-on-white fabric* (or off white-on-white) for top and backing: 4 yards, or 2 yards for the top and 2 yards for the backing

flannel for middle layer: 2 yards

white-on-white stripe or other contrasting fabric for double French fold binding: 1 yard

fabric marker (chalk, permanent pen, or pencil)

white to off-white threads: assortment of approximately 40 spools

*Look for a white-on-white fabric with a strong floral, geometric, or abstract design.

STEP 1

Cut the 4-yard piece of fabric into two 2-yard pieces (one for the top and one for the backing). Press both pieces and the flannel thoroughly.

STEP 2

Stack the layers, beginning with the backing fabric, placed right side down on a flat work surface. Carefully place the flannel on top, smoothing out any wrinkles. Place the top fabric right side up over the flannel. Smooth out any wrinkles to make sure the layers are not bunched up anywhere.

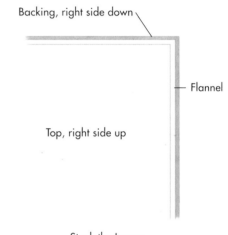

Backing, right side down

Flannel

Top, right side up

Stack the Layers

STEP 3

Choose a basting method and secure the three layers starting at one end: hand baste with water soluble thread, making lines of stitching about 8" apart vertically and horizontally, or use pins to hold all the layers together. To make sure the layers won't shift, also machine baste with water soluble thread by stitching down the middle of the coverlet both vertically and horizontally, then add a few more stitching lines in each direction to hold the layers together well.

STEP 15

Beginning with one of the scallops, pin the binding to the back of the coverlet, matching the raw edges of the binding and the quilt. Leave about 12" of the binding free at the beginning. Use a lot of pins to ease the binding along the curves. Continue pinning around all the sides of the quilt. Mark the spot where the two ends of the binding meet, open up the binding and connect the two ends with a diagonal seam, finger press the seam open, and refold the binding. Finish pinning the scallops.

STEP 16

Sew the binding to the coverlet with a ⅜" seam allowance. Lightly press the binding away from the coverlet. Trim the *binding* seam allowance to ¼" so the seam will lie flatter.

STEP 17

Turn the binding to the right side of the coverlet. Ease the binding in place, pulling out the curves with a pin point. Pin in place using a lot of pins. Baste the edge, removing the pins; this makes the topstitching straighter and keeps you from getting poked while sewing.

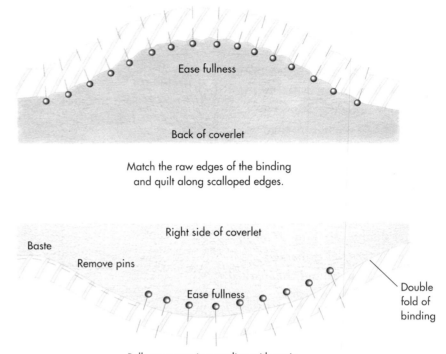

Ease fullness

Back of coverlet

Match the raw edges of the binding and quilt along scalloped edges.

Right side of coverlet

Baste

Remove pins

Ease fullness

Double fold of binding

Pull out curves in seamline with a pin

STEP 18

Using a matching thread, topstitch along the edge of the binding. Lightly press the edges. If the top is a little distorted from all the handling, or if the pressing took out some of the crinkle, spray the coverlet with a fine mist of water and toss it into the dryer for a few minutes to revive the crinkle in the coverlet.

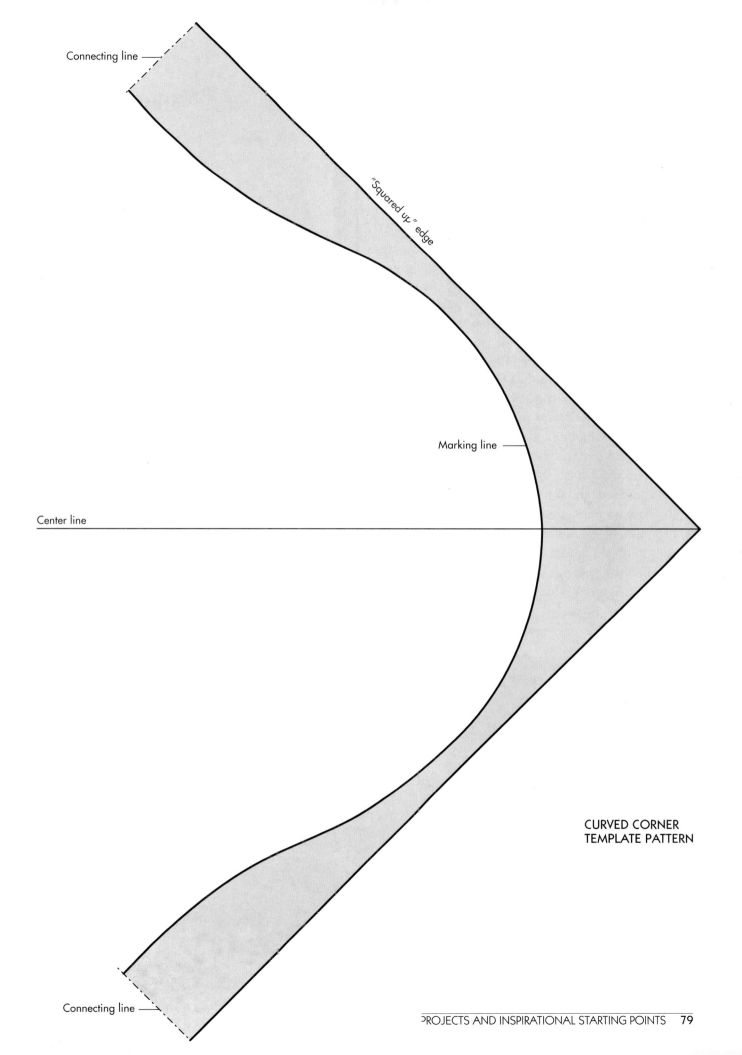

Connecting line

"Squared up" edge

Marking line

Center line

CURVED CORNER
TEMPLATE PATTERN

Connecting line

DOUBLE NINE-PATCH LAP QUILT

PROJECT

Method: raw-edge collage and weaving, with surface stitching through three layers

Stitch Style: straight and wavy pivots; wavy lines

This cuddly, warm lap quilt uses an assortment of thirty-six folk and plaid fabrics for the twelve different Double Nine-Patch blocks, with a contrasting border print and a plaid flannel on the back. I designed and made this quilt using the raw-edge collage and woven strips techniques. The individual squares which make up the blocks are cut in three different sizes; this way, the seams of the larger blocks are covered up by the next size smaller blocks that are layered on top. The quilt was surface stitched through all the layers, washed, dried, squared up, and bound using double French fold binding.

FACING PAGE: Double Nine-Patch Lap Quilt, 50½" x 64", Wendy Hill. Detail on page 41.

There are twelve different Double Nine-Patch blocks, six with prints in the plain squares (A blocks) and six with plaids in the plain squares (B blocks).

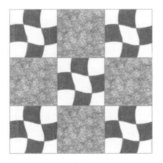

Block A

Block B

If you wish, you can simplify this by making two different repeat Double Nine-Patch blocks. Try other color combinations, such as florals, batiks, solid colors, or geometric prints to change the look of this traditional block.

SUPPLIES

woven squares: ¼ yard each of 24 different prints (12 light, 12 dark)

plain squares: ¼ yard each of 6 different plaids

plain squares: ¼ yard each of 6 different prints

outer border: 1 yard

plaid fabric for double French fold binding and bias trim: 1 yard

quilter's flannel for middle layer: 3¾ yard

backing (plaid or print flannel): 3¾ yard

fabric marking pen or pencil

thread: 40 assorted spools

water soluble basting thread

½" bias maker (optional)

STEP 1

Prepare the middle layer and backing first. Cut the quilter's flannel into two pieces, each 67½" long (1⅞ yard). Pin right sides together along the selvages, and sew with a ½" seam. Trim off the tightly woven edge of the selvages leaving at least a ¼" seam allowance. Press the seam open. Repeat with the backing fabric. Press the fabrics.

STEP 2

Draw a 5" layout grid onto the quilter's flannel using a clear, gridded ruler and fabric marking pen or pencil. Square up two sides (one short, one long) before drawing the first line. Starting about 8" from the cut edge on the short side, draw the first line from one side to the other. Continue drawing lines 5" apart, for a total of thirteen lines. Turn to the squared-up long side, start 8" from the cut edge, and draw the first line, using the lines of the gridded ruler to keep this new line at right angles to the cross lines. Continue drawing lines 5" apart, for a total of ten lines.

STEP 3

Stack the layers, beginning with the backing fabric placed right side down on a large, flat surface. Carefully place the quilter's flannel on top, with the grid design facing up, smoothing out any wrinkles.

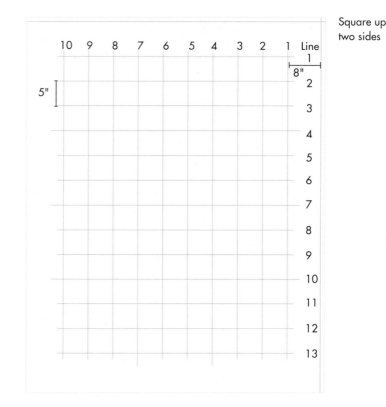

Layout Grid Diagram

STEP 4

Pin or hand baste with water soluble thread along the marked lines to hold the layers together. Select a thread which will blend with the backing fabric for the bobbin, and a contrasting top thread, and stitch along the marked lines. It is important to stitch as accurately as possible, because these lines are the guide for making the Double Nine-Patch blocks. Put this aside while you prepare the woven and plain blocks.

STEP 5

To make the woven squares, take the twenty-four light and dark fabrics, and pair up one light with one dark to make twelve pairs. Choose six pairs to make A blocks and six pairs to make B blocks.

STEP 6

Stack the pairs of fabrics with the dark piece on the bottom, right side up, and the light piece on top, right side up. Cut five 6" x 6" squares from all of the A block pairs of fabrics. Cut four 6" x 6" squares from all of the B block pairs of fabrics.

STEP 7

Line up one pair of fabrics at a time on the cutting mat, so that the square is within lines 6" apart. Using a rotary cutter, start at the bottom of the square and cut two wavy lines approximately 2" apart, stopping about ¼" from the top edge. (Use the lines of the mat as a guide. Since the lines are wavy, at some points the lines will be closer or farther than 2" apart.) Repeat with all twelve pairs of fabrics.

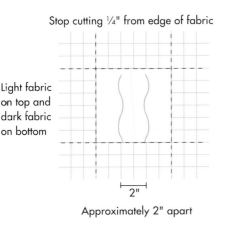

Stop cutting ¼" from edge of fabric

Light fabric on top and dark fabric on bottom

2"

Approximately 2" apart

STEP 8

The squares will be woven with a basic over, under weave. To weave the squares, lift the light square off the dark square, and set it aside. Lift up the middle strip of the dark square.

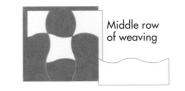

Wrong side

Right side up

Turn the light square clockwise, so the intact edge is on the right-hand side, and lay the top light strip over two of the dark strips, placing the light strip as close to the top as possible, right sides facing up.

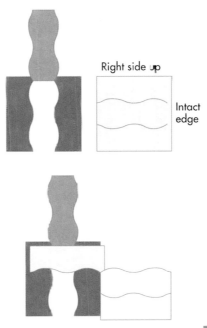

Right side up

Intact edge

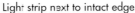

Light strip next to intact edge

Bring the middle dark strip down in place. The top row is now light, dark, light.

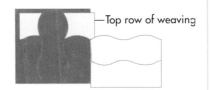

Top row of weaving

Weave the middle light strip "under, over, under." Snug up the middle row as close as possible to the top row. The middle row is now dark, light, dark.

Middle row of weaving

Weave the bottom light strip "over, under, over." Snug up the bottom row. The bottom row is now light, dark, light.

Finished Woven Block

Place a pin in each of the nine small squares, and machine baste with water soluble thread. (Note: the light and dark squares don't sit perfectly on top of each other because of the intact edges.)

Repeat with the remaining fifty-three squares.

TIP

Use the assembly line method to make this process go faster. Weave and pin the blocks first. Then machine baste all of the blocks.

STEP 9

To make the plain squares, cut four 6" x 6" squares from each of the six print fabrics. Cut five 6" x 6" squares from each of the six plaid fabrics. You are now ready to lay out the woven and plain squares.

STEP 10

Lay out the squares *on a design wall or large floor space* following the diagram, alternating A blocks with B blocks. Find a placement you like, but remember, the surface stitching will pull the colors of the quilt top together. Now it is time to trim the squares to size.

It is handy to be able to trim the squares and then place them *on the gridded middle/backing fabric.*

Unlike pieced blocks in which each block is made individually, with the raw-edge method the whole quilt top is created in one process.

STEP 11

First lay out all the 6" squares *on the gridded middle/backing fabric.* Overlap the extra ½" or so over the grid lines.

Follow the Cutting Guide and trim the appropriate squares to 5" x 6". These squares fit over the grid so the 6" side overlaps the grid line.

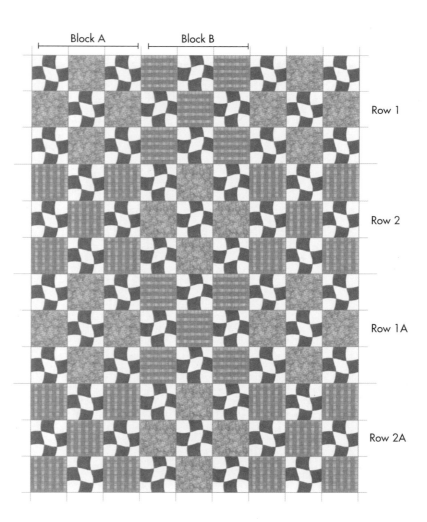

1	2	3
4	5	6
7	8	9

CUTTING GUIDE

Rows 1 & 1A

Block A:
6" x 6" for 1, 3, 7, 9
5" x 6" for 2, 4, 6, 8
5 " x 5" for 5

Block B:
6" x 6" for 2, 8
5" x 6" for 1, 3, 5, 7, 9
5" x 5" for 4, 6

Rows 2 & 2A

Block A:
6" x 6" for 5
5" x 6" for 2, 4, 6, 8
5" x 5" for 1, 3, 7, 9

Block B:
6" x 6" for 4, 6
5" x 6" for 1, 3, 5, 7, 9
5" x 5" for 2, 8

Block A   Block B

Row 1

Row 2

Row 1A

Row 2A

Next, trim the remaining squares to 5" x 5". These squares fit over the grid, finishing the remaining edges. To hold everything in place, secure the pieces in place with pins (placed every ½") or hand baste with water soluble thread.

STEP 12

Cut the border strips on the crosswise grain (from selvage to selvage); six strips, each 5" wide and two strips, each 5½" wide. Trim off the selvages and square up the ends.

Sew two 5" strips right sides together with a ⅜" seam allowance. Press the seam open. Repeat with the remaining three pairs of 5" and 5½" strips.

The bottom border is made with the 5½" wide strips. The bottom border is placed ½" under the cut edge of the blocks. The cut edge of the blocks lines up with the grid line, and overlaps the border fabric. Pin in place.

The remaining three border strips are overlapped over the block edges. Line up the top edge of the border strips with the grid lines on either end of the row, and check to make sure the cut edge is about 5" from the next line over. Pin in place. Repeat with the remaining borders.

½" Grid line

Border overlaps block edges

Grid line

First border

STEP 13

Use a thread color that blends with the backing and the top fabrics. Look for something neutral and flat, not shiny. Set the machine to make a narrow, open zigzag. Beginning with the outside edge of the border, zigzag each line that is 5" apart, both vertically and horizontally. Remove the pins.

STEP 14

Using the same or another neutral, blending thread, stitch in wavy lines both vertically and horizontally, catching the raw edges of the woven blocks as you sew. Another option would be to zigzag the raw edges of the woven squares, with straight stitched wavy lines between the squares. The extra time spent "nailing down" the raw edges and over-all layers will pay off in the next step.

STEP 15

Surface stitch the quilt top through all the layers, using any stitch style. Be sure to stitch all the way to the outside edges, or even a little beyond, for consistent density everywhere. Roll up the bulk of the quilt for easier handling.

STEP 16

Wash and dry the quilt. Press lightly as needed. Square up the sides.

STEP 17

Cut 1" strips on the bias from the bias trim fabric, to equal about 200". Cut the edges at a 45° angle, sew together with a ⅜" seam allowance, and press the seams open.

STEP 18

Make ½" bias trim with the 1" fabric using a bias maker (follow manufacturer's directions) or by pressing the sides ¼" to the middle.

STEP 19

Center and pin the bias trim over the seamline between the border and the inner quilt; fold a miter at the corners. Fold the two ends under where they meet. Topstitch along both edges of the trim.

STEP 20

Make double fold French binding with the same fabric to finish the outside edges of the quilt. Cut enough 3"-wide strips on the bias to make about 240". Cut the edges at a 45° angle, stitch together with a ⅜" seam allowance, and press the seams open. Fold the binding in half lengthwise and press. Pin binding to quilt with right sides together, connecting the ends to make a continuous strip and mitering the corners. Sew with a ⅜" seam allowance. Turn binding to the back, and hand sew in place.

COMING TO THE SURFACE: A CRAZY PATCH WALL QUILT

INSPIRATIONAL STARTING POINT

Method: whole cloth (pieced), surface stitching through three layers (pieced top, foundation, backing)

Stitch Style: improvisational

Kelly Simbirdi made this quilt after a "Color Impressions in the Crazy Quilt Technique" class with Diana Leone, author and owner of The Quilting Bee in Mountain View, California. Kelly used a whole-cloth variation with this surface-stitched wallhanging.

The quilt top was foundation pieced using a muslin foundation, then surface stitched. After washing, drying, and ironing, Kelly layered the quilt top with a backing fabric, and added more surface stitching to hold the layers together. She washed and dried the quilt again, squared up the edges, then finished it with a facing strip on the back of the quilt. Although there is no batting in this quilt, it has a hefty feel to it. Kelly cautions people about surface stitching in two stages as she did, because this quilt does not hang perfectly flat.

Coming to the Surface,
35½" x 30½", Kelly Simbirdi

Detail of Quilt

TWO GARDEN QUILTS

PROJECT

Method: raw-edge collage using geometric shapes, surface stitching through all the layers

Stitch Style: Through the Eyes of a Child, wavy lines; *Walkabout,* pivot stitch

Beginning with a vision of a flower garden with sunlight shining through it, Debra Wruck designed her quilt *Through the Eyes of a Child,* which she says took on a life of its own during the creative process.

The name was inspired by the feeling Debra had when looking at the quilt, imagining herself as a child again lying on the grass, looking up at the blooms. Debra took Best of Show at the Downieville Quilt Show in Downieville, California, in 1995, and won first place in the 1996 Nevada County Fair, California, in the wall quilt division, with this quilt. The judges especially liked the raw-edge construction and surface stitching.

FACING PAGE: Walkabout, 66" x 83", Wendy Hill

I designed and made *Walkabout* in 1992 while leading a workshop for a group of seven public school teachers who wanted to make their first quilt.

Over one hundred fabrics were precut into modular shapes and organized by color and texture: big and flashy; petite prints; pastels; texture and undergrowth; dead and dying; and two compelling colors—periwinkle blues and burnt oranges. Beginning with imagery of literal and metaphorical gardens, the teachers, each with their own grid paper on a design wall, created their own interpreta-

Through the Eyes of a Child, 24" x 33", Debra Wruck

tion of a garden. All the quilts were spectacular and different: a monochromatic leafy forest floor in browns; an English garden with vines wrapping around an archway; spiky sunflowers with shafts of sunlight; a Trip Around the World design with floral fabrics; and more. This was the first quilt in which I used that "stitching thing," as my husband called what later became known as surface stitching.

You can make your own garden quilt using raw-edge collage. Debra used a 1½" grid, with 2" x 2" cut squares to allow for the overlapping. My quilt is based on a 3½" grid, and modular units of squares, rectangles, and triangles, which fit together in a variety of ways.

SUPPLIES

assorted flowered, textured fabrics: total yardage equivalent to the number of yards for the middle layer fabric

middle layer: muslin, flannel, or low-loft batting the size of the quilt, plus 6"–8" extra in width and length

backing: same size as the middle layer fabric

water soluble glue stick or water soluble basting thread

thread: 20–30 assorted spools for a wallhanging, 40 for a twin bed size

.004 nylon monofilament thread: optional

fabric marker

STEP 1

Look for flowered, textured fabrics. It is helpful to take a cut-out cardboard window of the finished-size shape along with you to the fabric store. Place the window over fabrics to see what they will look like when cut up. Prints and designs which fill up and spill beyond the window will give a good effect in a garden quilt. Avoid fabric designs which fit neatly or repeat inside the window; the print is too small to give the desired effect.

STEP 2

Decide on the grid size you want to use. The smaller the wallhanging or quilt, the smaller the grid must be to create a picture. When using squares, the size of the grid may be as small as 1", but when using modular units, you'll want a grid size easily divided into subsections. A good grid size for modular units is 3"–4"; any larger and the quilt or wallhanging must be very large to accommodate the scale of the garden image. I used a 3½" grid for my quilt.

STEP 3

Make a grid on the muslin or flannel base fabric. Use a clear, gridded ruler and a fabric marker to draw the lines. Refer to page 41 for more detailed instructions. The important thing to remember is to make sure the first line is parallel to

the squared-up edge of the fabric panel; otherwise the grid can get very askew by the time you reach the other side. If you plan to surface stitch through all the layers of your quilt, stitch the gridded muslin or flannel to the backing fabric along the grid lines *before* you proceed to Step 4. If surface stitching just through the base fabric, continue to the next step.

STEP 4

Precut your fabric assortment and sort by value and color. Before you start cutting, plan ahead for how the pieces will be layed out. When using all squares, add a ¼" overlap to each side (½" total to each square), then overlap the pieces on the grid. For a "pieced" look with seams, be sure to overlap the pieces in all the same direction.

I used modular units in my quilt: one big square, four small squares, two rectangles, two big triangles, and four small triangles. I added ¼" around all of my modular shapes, and overlapped them randomly in various combinations.

The result is more painterly and less pieced looking, although many people don't realize it isn't pieced until they are up very close to the quilt.

Raw edges overlapped the same direction for a pieced look.

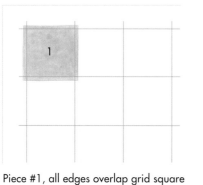

Piece #1, all edges overlap grid square

Piece #2, overlaps three sides

Piece #3, continue adding pieces

You'll get a more random look by overlapping the edges any which way.

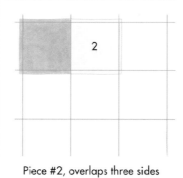

Piece #1, all edges overlap grid square

Piece #2, all edges overlap

Piece #3, overlaps three sides;
continue random overlapping

I added ¼" overlap to all of my modular shapes, and overlapped randomly for a painterly look.

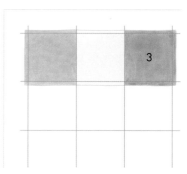

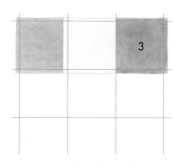

Triangle #1 overlaps #2

Piece #3 is tucked under first two triangles

Piece #4 overlaps piece #3

Same layout with pieces butted together for a pieced look.

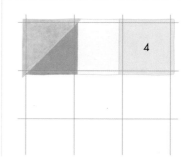

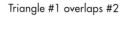

Cut pieces exact size. Butt together.

To make the modular units, review the general information in Chapter 4, page 40. For my quilt, start with a 3½" square (same size as the grid):

	General	**Example**	
	square finished size of square + $^1/_2$"	Cut a 4" square	
	rectangle Finished length of the square + $^1/_2$" x half the finished width + $^1/_2$"	Cut two 4" x 2$^1/_4$" rectangles	
	quarter square Half the finished size of the square + $^1/_2$"	Cut four 2$^1/_4$" x 2$^1/_4$" squares	
	half-square triangle Finished size of the square + $^7/_8$"	Cut a 4$^3/_8$" square Cut the square in half diagonally	
	quarter-square triangle Finished size of the square + 1$^1/_4$"	Cut a 4$^3/_4$" square Cut the square in quarters diagonally	

STEP 5

Using a design wall or a large flat surface, lay out the fabrics from your precut fabric palette. Debra used a piece of foamcore work board, which also allowed her to transport her work in progress for others to see. I used a design wall. Find a way to look at the quilt both up close and far away.

With garden quilts, value is just as important as color in how the fabrics create the scene. The best way to check for value placement is to take a black and white photograph of the layout. If this is not possible, try one of these ideas: turn off the lights; turn the piece upside down; look at the piece in a mirror; squint your eyes; take off your glasses; put on someone else's glasses; or look through a reducing lens or through binoculars backwards. Rework areas which look "solid" or those with hard lines.

STEP 6

When you have the layout you like, it is time to secure the surface. Use a water soluble glue stick to adhere the pieces to the grid, or hand baste with water soluble thread, or use lots of pins. See Securing the Layers on page 26 for a full discussion on these options.

Debra used pins, then zigzagged the edges both horizontally and vertically with monofilament thread. She planned to use a less dense stitch style of wavy lines, so she didn't want to use a blending thread color to zigzag, which might show up in the end result. I used pins, then zigzagged with a blending thread on the horizontal and vertical grid lines as well as the edges of the shapes.

STEP 7

Plan ahead to the finishing of the quilt before surface stitching. I surface stitched the inner garden first, then added the outer border of blue and black squares. I bound the outer edges of the quilt, turning the binding to the back of the quilt. Finally, I surface stitched the outer border.

Debra planned to bind her quilt with a double French fold binding, so she surface stitched the entire quilt top first. She wanted the binding to blend in with the rest of the quilt, so she pieced fabrics together to blend into the adjacent area of the quilt top.

Surface stitch using the stitch style of your choice. Both Debra and I used a collection of thread colors and fiber contents for each section of the quilt surface. Debra used all vertical wavy lines, allowing the curves to overlap each other. I used primarily straight pivot stitches of all different sizes, sweeping horizontally, vertically, and diagonally.

Both of us decided ahead of time not to wash our quilts, since neither wanted the "crinkle," just the texture of the thread. If you want the crinkle, wash and dry the quilt after surface stitching.

MIDNIGHT GARDEN
WALL QUILT

INSPIRATIONAL
STARTING POINT

Method: raw-edge collage, surface
stitching through three layers

Stitch Style: improvisational

Kazuko Dailey used random and
stylized shapes to make this
wallhanging. She surface stitched
a piece of purple background
fabric first. She added the border
strips, then stacked the layers
from the bottom up: backing
fabric right side down; muslin
middle layer; and purple fabric
right sides up. Working with a
"palette" of random shapes and a
design surface, Kazuko arranged
and scattered the fabrics until she
found a layout she liked, and
allowed the purple stitched
background to show through.
Spiral shapes, circular cutouts,
and other stylized shapes were
added on top. Kazuko connected
the layers with more improvisational surface stitching. The edges
were finished with a double
French fold binding.

Midnight Garden, 40" x 51", Kazuko Dailey.
Detail on page 45.

FLAT, FLUFFY, FLAT WALL QUILT

INSPIRATIONAL STARTING POINT

Method: raw-edge weaving, with surface stitching through a base fabric

Stitch Style: pivot; cross hatch

Kelly Simbirdi began weaving a series of original quilts and other things after taking a "Don't Piece It, Weave It" class with me in 1995. Named after the physical elements of the quilt, *Flat, Fluffy, Flat* won first place in the 1996 Marin Quilt and Needle Art Show in California.

Some people plan ahead when designing a quilt, but Kelly lets the piece evolve as she goes, and it works. This is good news for people who like to take an idea and start working, but Kelly reminds me she sometimes walks into problems by working this way. But, as many quilters have

Flat, Fluffy, Flat,
37½" x 32½",
Kelly Simbirdi

discovered, problems often lead to unexpected, innovative solutions. With this in mind, follow the steps Kelly used to make this quilt.

Kelly began weaving one fabric, cut into raw edge strips, over flannel. The fabric ranged through browns, grays, and blue grays, with a "zebra" or "mountainous" black stripe over the surface. She pin basted, then surface stitched with an assortment of surprising colors, including Halloween orange, which blends in very well.

Next, Kelly squared up the edges, impulsively cutting off the extra unwoven strips from one side only, for an asymmetrical look. In the meantime, she prepared two other panels. One was a hand quilted panel of golden colored fabric with a low-loft batting. The other was a piece of brown fabric sewn right sides together, pillow-case-style, with backing and flannel; this was turned right sides out, with the opening sewed closed and pressed flat.

For the assembly Kelly started with the flat brown panel, followed by the fluffy golden panel, with the flat, surface-stitched panel on top. Everything was great, except Kelly didn't like the asymmetrical look of the surface-stitched piece with fringe on only three sides. After two or three hours of struggling, and with the input of her mother, Kelly tried adding a replacement fringe with the gold and brown fabrics. It worked, and life was good again.

Detail of Quilt

THREE QUILTS, TWO BORDERS, AND A BINDING

INSPIRATIONAL STARTING POINT

Method: whole cloth (pieced), surface stitching through top layer

Stitch Styles: all—pivot stitch; *Funny Side Up* with "ee-ee"

Charlotte Patera and I used the whole-cloth method to create three different kinds of "finishing touches" for our quilts. This is a good example of the way surface stitching can be used in small amounts and be very effective.

BOX FRAME BORDER

Charlotte created an interesting textural border to accent her quilt, *Spirits of the Southwest.*

Charlotte began with a large rectangle of fabric and a water soluble stabilizer. To determine the length of the rectangle, measure the **longest** side of the quilt, including seam allowances, plus 4" for shrinkage.

*Note: If the **shortest** side of the quilt plus two times the border width including seam allowances plus 4" for shrinkage is longer than the above (first) measurement, use this second measurement for the length of the rectangle. (This will happen if the quilt is close to square.)*

To determine the width of the rectangle, take the desired width of each border, including seam allowances, times four for the four sides, plus 4" for shrinkage.

After surface stitching, washing, and drying, she continued to make her frame border as usual with her surface-stitched fabric, cutting the rectangle into strips and sewing them onto the quilt top, two opposite sides at a time.

Spirits of the Southwest, 21" x 25", Charlotte Patera, shown here courtesy of Ann Nickerson

Detail of Quilt

BOX FRAME BORDER WITH PILLOW CASE FINISHING

I added a surface-stitched frame border to my quilt, *Funny Side Up* using the pillowcase to finish the quilt.

I started with a rectangle, calculated the same way Charlotte did with her border. This was especially important since the surface stitching formed a pattern, which I wanted to be repeated on all four sides. I used a muslin base with the fabric for the surface stitching.

Instead of distributing all the thread colors, some colors were clustered in bands, with straight stitch variations for added texture. These bands of color and texture went across the rectangle, so when cut into strips, each strip had a cross section of the surface stitched pattern.

After washing and drying, I cut the fabric into strips. The strips were sewn to the quilt top using the box frame border method.

To assemble the quilt using the pillowcase method, cut the batting and backing a little larger than the quilt top. Stack the layers with the batting on the bottom, the quilt back right side up, and the quilt top right side down. Smooth the layers. Secure the layers with pins; mark the points to start and stop stitching with two pins, and pin every 2" in the area to be left open.

Sew the layers together using your allotted seam allowance included in the border. Trim the corners and seams. The batting may be cut close to the seamline; it is helpful to grade the seams, by keeping the backing a little wider than the quilt top.

Turn the quilt, pull out the corners, and smooth flat. Pin around the outside edge every 2–3" to help flatten the quilt. Hand sew the opening closed with a blind stitch. Hand or machine quilt as desired to hold the layers together. For *Funny Side Up*, I had already machine quilted the top before adding the back and batting. To hold the layers together I machine quilted with monofilament thread in the ditch, with matching thread for the backing fabric in the bobbin.

Funny Side Up, 33" x 33", Wendy Hill.
Detail of border on page 33.

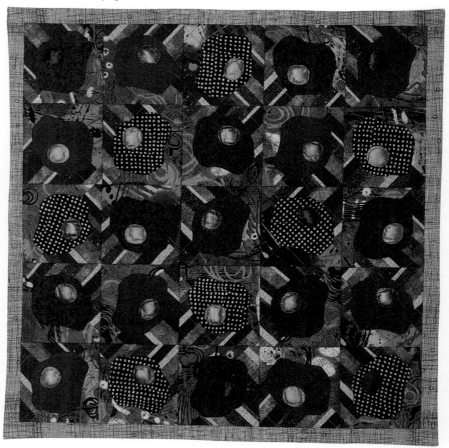

DOUBLE FRENCH FOLD BINDING

Charlotte surface stitched a "new" fabric to make the binding for her quilt *Spirits Over Santa Fe* .

Using fabric cut on the straight of the grain, Charlotte used the same method described for the box frame border on page 99 to calculate the size rectangle she needed for the binding. Layered with a water soluble stabilizer, she surface stitched with light colored threads to contrast with the blues and greens of the fabric. After washing and drying, Charlotte cut the fabric into 3"-wide strips to make the finished ½" binding.

Spirits Over Santa Fe, 25" x 28",
Charlotte Patera

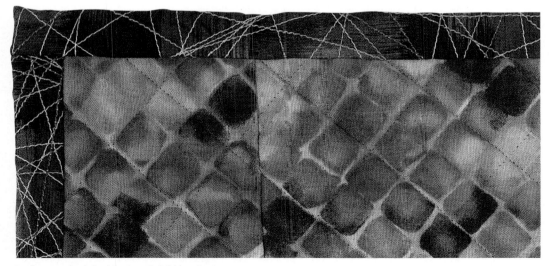

Surface stitched double French fold binding

CLOTHING

This section features clothing for adults and children primarily using commercial patterns, but other patterns may be used. Check your local retail outlet to purchase the patterns. A listing of the other commercial patterns is given in the Resources section on page 141. A few contributors used their own original patterns. For a more tailored look, and to make adjustments for a better fit; use a muslin dummy for the pattern. One project uses a purchased denim jumper; this can be adapted to any piece of purchased clothing. Be inspired by these photographs; surface stitching is an easy way to make your own one-of-a-kind wearable art.

FOUR WHOLE-CLOTH VESTS USING COMMERCIAL PATTERNS

PROJECT

Method: whole cloth, surface stitching through top layer

Stitch Style: straight and wavy pivot stitch; orange vest with over grid

TOP: By Wendy Hill, (Fashion Blueprints #402), note added piping

CENTER LEFT: By Katie Edwards, (Fashion Blueprints #402), note added piping

CENTER RIGHT: By Wendy Hill, (Fashion Blueprints #402); note flat bias trim

BOTTOM: By Wendy Hill, on loan from Sue Royston, (Fashion Blueprints #402), note flat bias trim

Although Katie Edwards and I both used the same commercial pattern by Fashion Blueprints to make our vests, this or any other pattern may be used. Since you are making "new" fabric, then assembling the pattern, there are no restrictions on the pattern style, other than using a pattern within your sewing ability.

These vests mix surface-stitched and plain fabric in the vest. The orange vest is made with one fabric, while the others use a contrasting fabric for the surface-stitched pieces. Two of the vests have added piping on the pockets and facings. The other two vests have a flat bias trim accenting the same places.

When making your own whole-cloth vest, plan to surface stitch just some of the pieces or all of them. Look for ways to enhance the pattern, such as piping, bias trim, or jewelry, as with these vests.

SUPPLIES

commercial pattern or your own design

fabric and water soluble stabilizer: amount required for pattern, plus extra fabric to allow 2" extra around each pattern piece

thread: 10–15 assorted spools

notions: as needed

STEP 1

Cut out the pattern pieces to be surface stitched, allowing 2" extra around the cutting lines. Use the cut-out fabric pieces as patterns to cut the water soluble stabilizer. As an alternative, you can group the pieces together in one or two big rectangles, allowing 1" between the pattern pieces and 2" around the outside perimeter. See Chapter 1, page 18, for special layouts.

STEP 2

Layer the fabric with the water soluble stabilizer. Make sure you have a right and a left side, especially when using a batik or dyed fabric, which may look the same on both sides. Secure with pins or hand or machine basting with water soluble thread.

STEP 3

Surface stitch using the stitch style you prefer. If the back of the surface-stitched fabric will not be seen when wearing the garment, use an economical thread for the bobbin. When stitching, be sure to distribute the same thread color and stitch style over all the pieces for a uniform look. This is usually desirable for mirror image pieces, such as front facings or arm facings. Discard this advice if you want an asymmetrical look, or if you want some pieces to look different from others, such as the front and the back, for example.

STEP 4

Wash and dry the surface-stitched pieces. If the other vest fabric hasn't been prewashed, do it now. Lightly press the surface-stitched pieces if needed.

STEP 5

Cut out all the vest pieces on the cutting lines. Make the vest following the pattern directions, adding any piping, bias trim or other accents if desired. Step-by-step pressing is important for making your garment look professionally made. To restore any crinkle lost through pressing, lightly mist with water and toss in the dryer for a few minutes.

BLACK, WHITE & RED JACKET/VEST AND HAT

INSPIRATIONAL STARTING POINT

Method: raw-edge woven strips, two layers (no base)

Stitch Style: improvisational

This is Sandy's first surface-stitched project. She used cotton and cotton blend fabrics with rayon and metallic threads. This garment is just two layers thick with the "over, under" of the woven strips. The hat was made in sections using woven leftovers and whole cloth.

Sandy cut her strips into a variety of widths. She started weaving the strips, pinning as she went, and stitching them together every 5" or 6" of weaving. Sandy kept adding to it until she had a piece big enough to cut out the pattern piece (with allowance for shrinking). Sandy says she surface stitched in straight lines, circles, fan tails, and "as the whim to change direction came upon me," using up some of her leftover thread stash.

She assembled the garment using raw-edge construction techniques (see Chapter 7, pages 120 and 121), with a bias binding to finish the outside edges. She also used raw-edge construction methods to assemble the hat, surface stitching the sections together until she had two sections of four each. She surface stitched these two sections together, then followed the pattern instructions to add the brim and line the cap.

By Sandy Wagner, (vest, Vogue #1985; hat, Kaleidoscope #204, Timber Lane Press), modeled by Rose Woodward

Detail of Vest

JUMPER WITH GATHERED TIERED SKIRT

INSPIRATIONAL STARTING POINT

Method: whole cloth, surface stitching through top layer

Stitch Style: pivot stitch

I made this jumper (below) using a commercial pattern (see Resources on page 141 for more pattern information).

Instead of piecing and appliquéing the jumper top, I surface stitched the jumper front and back. I also simplified the back bodice by cutting it out all in one piece, instead of putting together three pieces. The same fabric (unstitched) was used for the short, gathered ruffle accents on each tier of the skirt, making a contrast between the look of the plain and surface-stitched fabric.

By Heather Braley, (Folkwear Afgani Nomad Dress), modeled by Marta Woodward

DRESS WITH SURFACE STITCHED BODICE

INSPIRATIONAL STARTING POINT

Method: whole cloth, surface stitching through top layer

Stitch Style: pivot stitch

Heather Braley made her dress with a surface-stitched bodice. The mix of rayon (skirt, sleeves) and cotton fabrics (bodice, cuffs) along with the surface stitching allows this dress to go casual, or be "dressed up" with the surface-stitched clutch purse at night (see page 139).

To make your own dress or jumper using surface stitching, look for a pattern you like. Simple styling, with one-piece bodice fronts and backs, are the easiest to adapt to surface stitching. Layer the fashion fabric with muslin before surface stitching to add stability to the garment; eliminate any interfacing. Consider making a matching tote bag or clutch purse for an elegant or exclusive touch, while whipping up the garment.

By Wendy Hill, (Wild West jumper by k.p. kids & co.), modeled by Marta Woodward, The Peacock Inn, Grass Valley, California. Detail on page 30.

JACKET

INSPIRATIONAL STARTING POINT

Method: whole cloth, surface stitching with light-weight batting

Stitch Style: body—horizontal wavy lines; sleeve center—crosshatching; black band—straight and wavy pivot with over-grid

I adapted the pattern for this jacket (see Resources on page 141 for more pattern information).

I lengthened the pattern to hit just above the knees, lengthened the sleeves to my knuckles, omitted the cuffs and added ribbing cuffs, and made a separate lining.

For this jacket I made surface-stitched fabric at the same time I added an insulating layer of Thermore® by Hobbs. I cut out the pattern pieces, allowing 2" extra all the way around, from the fashion fabric, Thermore, and muslin. After layering and securing the pieces, I surface stitched the jacket body with wavy horizontal lines, the upper circular sleeve piece with crosshatching, and the black band with improvisational stitching and yellow over-grid. The remaining pieces were "quilted": the bodice front and back with

diagonal lines about 1" apart, and the lower sleeve with free-motion meandering. All the pieces were washed and dried, along with the lining fabrics.

I assembled two jacket bodies: the outside fashion fabric side and the lining. For fun, I used three different fabrics for the lining, although I have to fling the jacket wide open for anyone to see it. All seams were pressed open to reduce bulk. To finish the jacket the lining was placed right sides together with the outside body, pinned, and sewn around the outside edge, leaving an opening for turning right sides out. Once turned, the opening was hand sewn closed and the sleeves finished with the ribbing cuffs.

Make your own jacket with surface stitching and low-loft batting. With washing and drying there is not as much crinkle with the batting, and the fabric is somewhat firm. Choose a pattern which doesn't require a lot of drape and is meant to be warm. The batting really makes the jacket comfortable in cold weather.

By Wendy Hill, (Bubble Wrap Coat #202 by Shirley Fowlkes), modeled by Marta Woodward, car courtesy of Doug and Linda Stubbs

PURCHASED DENIM JUMPER

INSPIRATIONAL STARTING POINT

Method: whole cloth to make surface stitched appliqué fabric

Stitch Style: crosshatch

We don't always have time to sew our clothes from scratch, but this doesn't have to prevent us from using surface stitching to create unique art-to-wear. I appliquéd geometric shapes cut from surface-stitched fabric to transform this denim jumper from something nice to something fabulous.

I shopped for something in denim: a jacket, dress, shirt, or jumper with simple open spaces conducive for appliquéing. Many items initially looked good, but a closer look revealed topstitching or pieced bodices which would compete with the appliqué shape. I also needed a style which would allow me room to get in with the sewing machine and sew. Clothing with fitted sleeves seemed to have too small a work area for comfortable sewing. This jumper met all the criteria: made of denim; one-piece bodice front and back; open area to work with the sewing machine.

I picked up a red tee shirt to go with the jumper, but I wanted to stay away from a red, white, and blue combination with the surface-stitched fabric. I found a multicolored fabric with warm reds and golds and cool blues and greens. A collection of thread colors picked from the fabric made the surface stitching meld with the fabric colors. The appliqué shapes are based on traditional quilting designs. I took advantage of the negative space of the jumper to make a "square within a square" pattern on the back and a strip of wild goose chase on the front.

By Wendy Hill, modeled by Marta Woodward at The Peacock Inn, Grass Valley, California

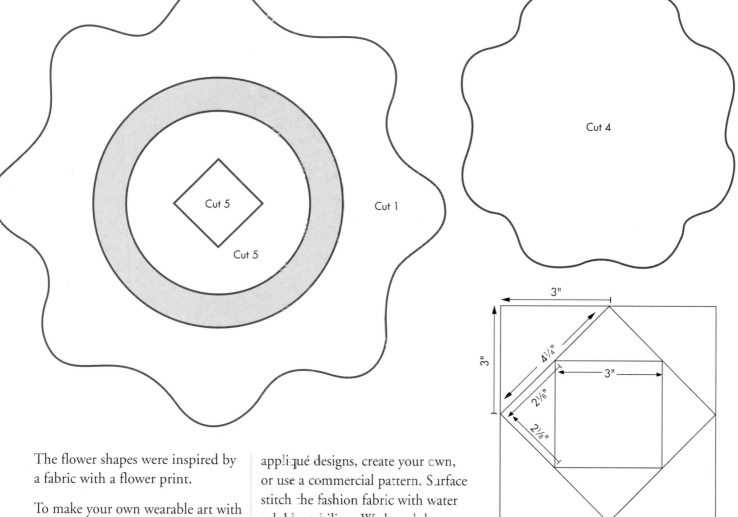

Cut 4

Cut 1

Cut 5

Cut 5

3"

3"

4¼"

2⅛"

2⅛"

3"

6"

The flower shapes were inspired by a fabric with a flower print.

To make your own wearable art with a purchased garment, use my appliqué designs, create your own, or use a commercial pattern. Surface stitch the fashion fabric with water soluble stabilizer. Wash and dry, then cut out the appliqué designs.

FIVE RAW-EDGE COLLAGE VESTS USING COMMERCIAL PATTERNS

PROJECT

Method: raw-edge collage, reversible, surface stitching through all the layers

Stitch Style: all pivot except turquoise by Ann–improvisational

Five women made five vests using five patterns and five color schemes. They all share raw edges, random shapes, and crinkly texture for an easy, wearable art garment. All of these vests can be worn on the reverse side, and were assembled using raw-edge construction methods. An alternative is to follow the pattern directions for conventional construction methods, but the vest won't be reversible.

Look for patterns with straight side seams, no darts, simple lines, and no pockets. The instructions are for surface stitching the two fronts and back separately, but the pattern pieces could be overlapped at the side or shoulder seams into one big piece; this will change the cutting layout and possibly the amount of required fabric for the lining and optional middle layer (see Chapter 1, page 18).

Any color scheme works. Fran Andre and I selected colors next to each other on the color wheel. I used light blues, lavenders, and pinks (tints of blue, purple, and red) for a "color saturated" pastel mix. Fran mixed different values of blues, blue-violets, and purples for her vest. Ann also used blues and greens found next to each other on the color wheel, with a little red-orange as an accent color. She created an underwater look with sparkle. Fall colors mix together in Kazuko's vest, with red-violet accents. Christine used opposites on the color wheel for a predominant mix of red-oranges and blue-greens, with black and white graphic prints for an accent. The mix of thread colors in the surface stitching unites just about any fabric mix.

SUPPLIES

commercial vest pattern

fabric: assortment of at least six fabrics, equal to at least the amount required for pattern

lining: amount required for pattern, plus extra fabric to allow 2" extra around each pattern piece

muslin, flannel, or low-loft batting for middle layer: same amount as lining (optional)

thread: 12-15 assorted spools

notions: as needed

UPPER LEFT: By Christine Barnes

UPPER RIGHT: By Wendy Hill, (Butterick #4384) on loan from Laura Clark

CENTER: By Fran Andre, (Kwik Sew #2209)

LOWER LEFT: By Kazuko Dailey, (modified Simplicity #9630)

LOWER RIGHT: By Ann Sanderson

STEP 1

Cut out lining and optional middle layer, adding 2" all the way around pattern pieces.

STEP 2

Press fabrics one last time. Tack lining to optional middle layer with water soluble glue or basting thread.

STEP 3

Cut out small, medium, and large random shapes from each fabric with scissors or rotary cutter and mat. For a reference (but not law), small shapes are approximately 2" by 3", medium 3" by 4", and large 4" by 5". For even distribution, sort the cut shapes into four piles, two for the back and one each for the fronts (for detailed information, see Chapter 4, page 38).

STEP 4

Working with one pattern piece at a time, scatter the shapes over the surface. Don't fret about exact placement while "playing" with the layout. When the fabric arrangement looks good to you (and the lights and darks, colors, and sizes are balanced with each other), start placing the pieces so the raw edges overlap about ¼". It is okay to overlap more, or to trim a shape to overlap closer to ¼". Pin in place for now. Repeat with the other pattern pieces.

STEP 5

Give the pieces a final check before committing to this arrangement. If possible, pin the pieces on a wall, and look at them up close and from across the room. If satisfied, baste in place using lots of pins, water soluble glue stick, water soluble basting thread, or sandwich a sheet of water soluble stabilizer across the top of each piece.

STEP 6

Surface stitch with your favorite stitch style combination. Wash, dry, and lightly press if needed.

STEP 7

Cut out the pattern pieces on the cutting line. Decide if you'll use conventional or raw-edge construction methods.

STEP 8

For conventional construction methods, follow the pattern directions. Consider using some kind of seam finish, such as binding, serging, or flat felling, for a more professional look. If the pattern uses a facing to finish the sleeve and outer edges, make this out of unstitched matching fabric. Or finish the sleeve and outer edges in one of the ways listed in Step 10.

STEP 9

For raw-edge construction, overlap the side and shoulder seams along the seamline. Stitch down the middle with a blending thread. Choose one of the following: trim the seam allowances to ⅜", and add some more surface stitching to tack down the edges; or cover the seam allowances with a raw edge strip of fabric, overlapped 2" squares, or leftover overlapped random shapes, and surface stitch in place.

STEP 10

To finish the sleeve and body outer edges, stitch ⅛" beyond the seam allowance from all the raw edges. For example, if the seam allowance is ⅝", stitch ¾" from the edges. Trim the seam allowance off the outer edges.

Choose one of the following edge finishes: leave raw, as is; serge the edges; bind with a raw-edge or folded-edge binding; cover the raw edges with leftover random shapes and surface stitch in place; or cover the raw edges with overlapped 2" squares (use smaller squares if needed to curve around the edge).

Add a decorative closing in front, or cinch up in back as Ann and Fran did with their vests.

GIRLS' JUMPER

INSPIRATIONAL STARTING POINT

Method: pin woven appliqué heart with whole cloth apron trim

Stitch Style: straight and wavy pivot; wavy lines

By Wendy Hill, (Blooming Baby Boutique, by k.p. kids & co.), modeled by Cailin Sakaue, Dow Alexander Memorial Park, Grass Valley, California

I used a pattern given in the Blooming Baby Boutique collection by k.p. kids and co.

A few extra touches and not much extra time make this very cute pattern a little more special for the little girl who receives it.

I used the same heart appliqué pattern I drew for the overalls (page 45), but this time I used pinweaving with a water soluble stabilizer "sandwich" to create the appliqué. I included a variety of ribbons, rickrack, and bias strips of the dress fabric in the pinweaving

design. To make the heart stand out more, I outlined it with a self-made bias trim from the pink check apron fabric.

To accent the apron bottom, I pieced a strip of rectangles together as the pattern called for, allowing extra for shrinkage. I surface stitched the pieced strip with a water soluble stabilizer, cut it to size, then continued with the pattern directions. A rainbow rickrack was added on the seamline as an accent.

Detail of Heart   Detail of Apron Bottom

BAMBOO SHIRT

INSPIRATIONAL STARTING POINT

Method: raw-edge collage with folk motifs and weaving, surface stitching through two layers plus shapes

Stitch Style: improvisational

I used the Bamboo Shirt pattern from the Sewing Workshop in San Francisco, California (see Resources on page 141 for more information).

After searching for just the right plaid fabric, I realized no one plaid was enough. With a little experimentation I decided to use eight plaids altogether.

I cut out my own folk-shaped stars, trees, fish, houses, and a moon from folk plaid and print fabrics. Use my designs, or make up your own.

Don't strive for accuracy when cutting out the shapes; irregularities add to the charm of these motifs.

Look for a shirt, jacket, or dress pattern with a place to cluster the shapes for surface stitching. I cut slits in a plaid base fabric to add areas of weaving, then clustered the folk shapes around the woven areas (refer to Chapter 5, page 55). To simplify the process, skip the weaving step. The optional zigzag around the raw edges wasn't practical with the dozens of shapes. Instead, catch a few raw edges as you surface stitch with each thread color, eventually catching most of the edges.

I washed the surface-stitched piece along with the plaid fabrics, then followed the pattern directions to assemble the shirt. The buttons, by polymer clay artist Dede Leupold, pick up the plaid and folk shape motifs of the shirt (see Resources on page 141).

By Wendy Hill, (Bamboo Shirt by The Sewing Workshop), modeled by Marta Woodward, in the Gold Country, California

Detail of Buttons

HAIKU JACKET
AND PLAID DRESS

INSPIRATIONAL STARTING POINT

Method: Jacket; raw-edge motifs, weaving, and whole cloth/new fabric; Dress; whole cloth/new fabric

Stitch Style: pivot; wavy lines; crosshatch

By Wendy Hill, (Haiku Jacket by The Sewing Workshop, dress McCalls #8149), modeled by Marta Woodward, in the Gold Country, California

I put together the Haiku Jacket pattern by the Sewing Workshop and dress by McCalls #8149 for an outstanding ensemble.

This outfit shows the many ways surface stitching can be used to achieve different looks. The plaid fabric is lightweight and tightly woven; with surface stitching it is very pliable and lightly crinkled. The linen fabric of the jacket

didn't crinkle much with surface stitching, but the thread texture shows up well on the fabric. The coarsely woven floral fabric on the collar and cuffs looks like a tapestry fabric with the surface stitching and shrinking.

Detail of Jacket

The floral and plaid fabrics were stitched with water soluble stabilizer to make new fabric. Extra floral fabric was used to accent the pocket and sleeve facing. I added extra design touches by placing the pocket reinforcement rectangles on the outside of the jacket (instead of the inside), using the contrasting plaid (see page 21).

I also modified the dress facing and put it on the outside (instead of inside) to make a bias trim around the neck.

A strip of linen was added to accent the bottom of each sleeve.

The jacket front features a folded collar. I cut the front larger to account for shrinking, and added a lattice of plaid woven tubes, scattered with raw-edge cutout flower motifs from the floral fabric. After surface stitching, washing, and drying, a bias strip of plaid covers the edge of the surface-stitched band, also adding a decorative touch.

With a little advance planning and surface stitching, this jacket and dress became outstanding and unique. Look for ways to include surface stitching and decorative touches on your next outfit.

Detail of Dress

FOUR WOVEN VESTS USING COMMERCIAL PATTERNS

PROJECT

Method: raw-edge woven strips for an optional reversible vest

Stitch Style: orange vest with wavy lines; others straight and wavy pivot

Three women made four vests using two different patterns. Use Ghee's "Linda's Vest #693," or your own favorite pattern. Look for patterns with straight side seams, no darts, simple lines, and no pockets. The instructions are for surface stitching the two fronts and back separately, but the pattern pieces could be overlapped at the side or shoulder seams into one big piece; this will change cutting layout and possibly amount of required fabric for lining and optional middle layer (see Chapter 1, page 18–19).

UPPER LEFT: By Wendy Hill, (Ghee's—Linda's Vest #693)

UPPER RIGHT: By Lorraine Kelly (Ghee's—Linda's Vest #693)

LOWER LEFT: By Christine Barnes

LOWER RIGHT: By Lorraine Kelly, (Ghee's—Linda's Vest #693)

CHRISTINE'S LINED WOVEN VEST

Christine Barnes was inspired by a madras plaid and a decorator fabric in fresh, clear colors for her woven vest. Christine kept the decorator print strips in order when she cut the 3" wide strips. The plaid strips, in various widths, were cut on the bias. She surface stitched through a muslin base making "new" fabric, then lined the vest with a silky fabric.

For this vest, only the fronts are surface stitched. If desired, use weaving, whole cloth, or raw-edge collage and surface stitch the back as well. The vest is constructed using conventional methods, following the pattern directions.

SUPPLIES

commercial pattern

contrasting fabrics for warp and weft on vest front: double the amount required for the pattern, plus extra fabric to allow 2" extra around each pattern piece

fashion fabric for unstitched vest back: amount required for pattern

lining for unstitched fronts and back: amount required for pattern

muslin or water soluble stabilizer for surface-stitched pieces: amount required for pattern, plus extra fabric to allow 2" extra around each pattern piece

thread: 12-15 assorted spools

STEP 1

Cut out the vest front pattern pieces from muslin or water soluble stabilizer, allowing 2" extra all the way around. Or, to make sure the vest fronts are identical, cut out one big rectangle large enough for both fronts, with the extra 2" around the outside edge. Cut warp and weft strips 2"–3" wide across the width of the fabric.

STEP 2

Lightly tape the muslin or stabilizer base to a flat work surface. Place the warp strips over the base, side by side, taping along the top edge. (If making individual vest fronts, work one at a time.)

STEP 3

Beginning at the top, weave the weft strips using a basic "over, under" pattern. Use a clear, gridded ruler to make sure the strips are at right angles to each other, by lining up the strips with the printed horizontal and vertical lines on the ruler. Weave the entire surface.

STEP 4

Secure using pins, basting, or sandwiching with another piece of water soluble stabilizer. Repeat with the other front.

STEP 5

Surface stitch with any stitch style. Wash and dry the woven surface with other fabrics for the vest. Lightly press if needed.

STEP 6

Cut out the vest fronts from the woven surface and the remaining pattern pieces for the back and lining. Assemble the vest following the pattern directions.

LORRAINE'S REVERSIBLE VESTS WITH LINING

Lorraine Kelly made her vests reversible by weaving over a muslin base and lining, surface stitching through all the layers, then using raw-edge construction methods to assemble the vests.

The optional middle layer of muslin makes the vest a little sturdier; omit for more drape. Follow Lorraine's lead and surface stitch whole-cloth fashion fabric for the back (layered with muslin and lining), or weave the back as well.

SUPPLIES

commercial pattern

contrasting fabrics for warp and weft for vest front: *double* the amount required for the pattern, plus extra fabric to allow 2" extra around each pattern piece

muslin for middle layer: amount required for pattern, plus extra fabric to allow 2" extra around each pattern piece (optional)

lining: amount required for pattern, plus extra fabric to allow 2" extra around each pattern piece

thread: 12-15 assorted spools

bias binding: optional

STEP 1

Cut out front and back pattern pieces from lining and optional muslin, adding 2" all the way around. Cut 2"- to 3"-wide strips for the warp and weft across the width of the fabric.

Follow steps 2, 3, 4, and 5 for Christine's Lined Woven Vest to weave and surface stitch the vest pieces, but stack the layers to include the lining.

STEP 6

Cut out the vest fronts and back on the pattern cutting lines.

STEP 7

To assemble the vest, overlap the side and shoulder seams on the seamlines. Stitch down the middle using a blending thread color. Trim the seams to ⅜". Surface stitch seams in place or cover with leftover raw-edge fabric strips or overlapped 2" squares. Surface stitch the fabrics in place, blending with previous surface stitching.

STEP 8

Stitch around the outside edges of the sleeve and body along the seamlines plus ⅛". Trim off the seam allowance and finish with a raw-edge or conventional binding; or cut off seam allowance and cover with overlapped 2" squares.

WENDY'S TWO-LAYER WOVEN VEST

I also made my vest reversible, but just two fabric layers thick, and the resulting vest is very flexible. I used lightweight batik and dyed fabrics, so the reverse side is just as colorful as the outside.

I also made my vest in one piece, by overlapping the side seams of the pattern ahead of time and weaving one big rectangle, making a "new" fabric. The shoulder seams were overlapped and surface stitched, and the edges finished with a bias binding.

SUPPLIES

commercial pattern

fabric for warp strips: a rectangle large enough to fit the back and fronts with side seams overlapped, and extra fabric to allow 2" extra around each pattern piece

fabrics for weft: an assortment equal to the size rectangle for the warp

water soluble stabilizer: same amount as rectangle for warp strips

fabric for outside edge bias binding: ½ yard *or* purchased bias binding

thread: 12-15 assorted spools

STEP 1

Trace the vest front onto paper. Overlap the side seams of the pattern; pin or tape in place. Refer to pages 18–19.

STEP 2

Lay out the vest pattern (now one piece) on the warp fabric. Allow at least 2" all the way around the pattern, *but cut the fabric into one big rectangle.*

(Weaving a rectangle is easier than weaving a big pattern shape, but it does result in leftover pieces.)

Cut out the water soluble stabilizer the same size as the warp rectangle.

STEP 3

Using a rotary cutter and a mat, cut the warp strips in the rectangle, running from the bottom of the vest up to the top. Leave the top edge intact by stopping ¼" to ½" from the edge. I cut freehand wavy strips, approximately 2" wide, moving the mat as needed to cut the entire rectangle. If you prefer, use a clear, gridded ruler and cut straight, measured strips.

STEP 4

I used two fabrics in the weft, but any number of fabrics may be used. Cut the weft strips 2" wide the width of the fabric, as I did, to get a "boxy" look, or vary the width to get irregular shaped rectangles in the weave.

STEP 5

Stack the layers and secure the warp. First, place the water soluble stabilizer on a flat work surface, and tape down in a few places. Next, lay the cut rectangle (warp) over the stabilizer, lining up the intact top edge with the stabilizer. Tape the intact edge to the flat surface. Straighten up the warp strips. Either tape the warp strips at the bottom or leave hanging loose (see Chapter 5, page 51).

STEP 6

I used two weft strips of one fabric, then one weft of the second fabric, using the basic "over, under" weaving pattern. If the warp strips are taped down, it's okay to start anywhere, but if the warp strips are loose, start at the top, intact edge, and work down. Weave the weft strips until the rectangle is completely woven.

STEP 7

Secure the layers using pin basting, or hand baste with water soluble thread. It's also possible to sandwich the woven surface with another rectangle of water soluble stabilizer on top, lightly pin baste, then machine baste with water soluble thread. In the beginning this kind of woven surface is very fragile, since there is nothing to hold it together; don't try to skimp on this step.

STEP 8

Surface stitch using any stitch style. Wavy lines in the surface stitching go well with wavy cut strips. Wash, dry, and lightly press if needed.

STEP 9

Lay out the vest pattern, lining up the grainlines with the warp strips. Cut out the vest pattern.

STEP 10

To assemble the vest, overlap the shoulder seams on the seamlines. Stitch down the middle using a blending thread color. Trim the seams to ⅜"; add a little more surface stitching to hold the seams in place, blending in the stitching with the previous stitching.

STEP 11

Stitch around the outside edges of the armhole and body along the seamline plus ⅛". Trim off the seam allowance. Add a raw-edge or conventional bias binding around the outside edges.

HONG KONG VEST AND PANEL PANTS

INSPIRATIONAL STARTING POINT

Method: vest: weaving and raw-edge collage; pants: weaving

Stitch Style: pivot, wavy lines, "ee-ee"

By Wendy Hill, (Hong Kong Vest and Panel Pants by The Sewing Workshop), modeled by Marta Woodward, Dow Alexander Memorial Park, Grass Valley, California

I made this outfit using an assortment of batik fabrics, using the Hong Kong Vest and Panel Pants patterns from The Sewing Workshop (see Resources on page 141 for more information). The pants are quite full through the knees, and lightweight, drapey fabrics make the pants more fluid. Although not reversible, I wanted the inside of the vest to have the finished look which can be achieved by using a dyed fabric (instead of a print). After manipulating and surface stitching the various pattern pieces to make "new" fabric, I followed the pattern directions to construct the clothing (with the exception of making the "knee patches" asymmetrical).

For the woven vest front and knee patches, I wove the strips over a water soluble stabilizer base. The vest uses wavy warp strips in the warp and straight-cut weft strips. The wavy warp strips run parallel to the grainline of the pattern. The knee patches use straight-cut weft strips in an assortment of widths.

Detail of Pants

The collaged stars on the left side of the vest use a variation of reverse appliqué discussed in Chapter 3, page 35. I cut two left vest fronts (one from each of the darker and lighter fabrics used) both right side up, allowing 2" for shrinkage around the pattern piece. I drew a five-point star shape in two sizes, and reproduced the design to make about fifteen stars total.

The stars were laid out across the left darker fabric front (the one which would be on the outside), until a preferred arrangement was found. I taped the stars in place, then carefully cut around them through the dark fabric only with a rotary cutter and mat. Next, I layered the dark fabric on top of

the lighter fabric and pin basted the two fronts together. The light-colored fabric showed through the star holes.

To make a star design on the back of the left front, I used the star cutouts from the darker fabric. I taped the vest to the window with the outside facing the window (but a light table could be used also). This let light in through the star holes so I could see where to place the star cutouts. I matched the cutout to the hole, gluing the star in place with water soluble glue stick. I zigzagged around each star with a blending thread, catching the raw edges on both sides.

FOR THE HOME

Surface stitching can be used when making all kinds of things for the home. In addition to placemats, pillows, and other "home decorator" kinds of items, consider making covered photo frames, greeting cards, and much, much more. Before tackling that next project on your list, ask if surface stitching would add to the delight of the finished item.

WOVEN PLACEMATS WITH NAPKINS & NAPKIN RINGS

PROJECT

Method: placemat: weaving raw-edge strips; napkin rings: whole cloth, one layer with stabilizer

Stitch Style: pivot and wavy lines

I designed these placemats to use on a bright summer day on the patio with a bouquet of fresh cut flowers from the garden. You can also make just one mat to use as a special accent on a table or chest.

I achieved the watery, blurred woven look (with no clear checkerboards) by choosing two big, splashy prints; one underwater fish print and one umbrella motif print, in related color schemes. The two fabric designs complement each other, but the pattern is lost when woven together. For more contrast (and visible checkerboards) choose two fabrics which contrast in color, pattern, and/or value.

I stacked the lining, muslin, and woven top together for the placemats and surface stitched through all the layers. (You will have fewer thread changes if you surface stitch the placemats and napkin rings all at one time.) After squaring up the mats I had the idea to add the "fringe" on the short sides, which added more texture to the finished mats. This is a good example of how inspiration can strike during the process of making something. Reversible matching napkins with surface-stitched napkin rings accent the placemats beautifully.

SUPPLIES

warp fabric: 1 yard (four 16" x 22" pieces)

weft fabric: 1 yard (four 16" x 22" pieces)

backing: 1 yard (four 16" x 22" pieces)

muslin middle layer: 1 yard (four 16" x 22" pieces)

contrasting fabric for binding: ½ yard

optional fringe: 9" x 12" of about 16 assorted fabrics (or ⅓ yard each of four fabrics)

thread: 14 to 16 assorted spools

water soluble basting thread

FACING PAGE: By Wendy Hill, Woven Placemats with Napkins & Napkin Rings, 12" x 18" (plus fringe)

STEP 1

Follow the measurements in the supply list and cut all the required fabrics. Prepare the double French fold binding by cutting 2⅛" bias strips, cutting the ends at 45° angles, piecing together, and folding in half lengthwise. Set aside.

STEP 2

Cut the warp and weft fabrics into 2" strips. It is very important to cut the warp fabric parallel to the 16" side and the weft fabric parallel to the 22" side. You will have eleven 2" warp strips and eight 2" weft strips for each mat. Press and set aside.

Warp fabric

Weft fabric

STEP 3

Press all the fabrics. Stack the layers for the placemats with the backing fabric right side down on a flat surface. Layer with the muslin, smoothing out any wrinkles. Set aside.

STEP 4

Place one of the placemats on the flat surface in front of you. Lay out eleven of the warp strips across the muslin, adjusting so that the edges butt up against each other. Pin about 3" from the top edge, using one pin per strip.

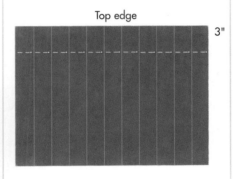

Top edge

STEP 5

Starting at the top (above the pins), weave the first weft strip in a simple plain weave (over, under). Using the pins on each warp strip, secure the first weft strip in place with a pin in each square.

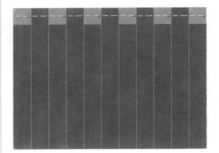

STEP 6

Continue weaving until all eight weft strips have been used. Pin baste using a pin in each square (or use more pins if desired).

STEP 7

Machine baste using water soluble basting thread, following the strips in the warp and weft. Zigzag the raw edges if desired with a blending thread.

STEP 8

Repeat Steps 3–6 for the remaining three placemats.

STEP 9

Surface stitch using pivots and wavy lines as I did, or your own combination of stitch styles. Remember to catch the raw edges when the opportunity arises, especially if there is no zigzagging. Spread each thread color over all of the placemats. Wash and dry; lightly press if necessary.

STEP 10

Square up the placemats to 12" x 18". Pin and sew the double French fold binding to the front of the placemat, right sides together with a ¼" seam allowance, folding mitered corners and joining the ends of the binding with a 45° angle seam (to reduce bulk). Lightly press toward the outer edge.

Fold the binding to the back, finishing the folded mitered corners, pinning in place so that the binding overlaps slightly with the seamline of the binding.

If not adding the fringe, finish the placemats by either hand stitching the binding in place with a slip stitch, or by machine sewing along the edge of the binding from the front. I top-stitched using a variegated rayon to add more color and texture.

If adding the fringe, hand baste the binding in place with regular basting thread. Set the mats aside and proceed to the next step.

STEP 11

To make the fringe, pair up two different 9" x 12" pieces of fabric, wrong sides together. Pin in two or three places. Repeat to make eight pairs of fabrics.

The stitching lines run parallel to the 9" sides of the pieces. Start by sewing a line of stitching about ⅛" from the edge. The next line is stitched about ⅜" from the previous line. The next line is ⅛" from the previous line. Continue alternating ⅜" with ⅛" across the fabric to the other side.

To avoid measuring, I used my presser foot as a guide. The stitching does not need to be precise, just fairly straight. Each 9" x 12" piece yields about 24 fringes, and each placemat requires about 48 fringes. If you get less than 24, just make some more.

Repeat the stitching lines on all eight pairs of fabric pieces.

STEP 12

To cut the fringe apart, line up a clear, gridded ruler inside the ⅛" space made by the stitching lines. Cut with a rotary cutter and mat. Repeat with the remaining stitched pieces of fabric.

STEP 13

Make a knot at both ends of each fringe. To keep the knots near the ends of the fringe, don't pull the knot tight until the loop of the knot is positioned near the end.

Fold each knotted fringe in half at an angle, so the inside of the fringe shows. Pin and set aside. Repeat with all the fringes.

STEP 14

Make eight piles of pinned, knotted fringes. I made my fringe with a variety of fabrics, so I distributed the different fabrics by sorting them into piles. Each pile will have about 24 fringes.

Take two piles and one placemat at a time. On the back of the placemat, pin the fringes along the 12" sides, with the fold extending past the edge of the binding by a scant ⅛", and pinning in place. Butt the fringes together, crowding them a little bit, but not overlapping them as they sit next to each other. Flip the placemat over to check the color assortment and placement. Repeat with the remaining three mats.

STEP 15

Topstitch the binding in place from the front of the placemats, sewing over the pinned fringes, using a blending or contrasting thread. If sewing over pins is a problem, try using masking tape to hold the fringes in place. After sewing the binding in place, carefully tear the masking tape away.

⅛" from edge

9"

⅜"   ⅛"   12"

MATCHING REVERSIBLE NAPKINS AND RINGS

SUPPLIES

side one of napkins: ¾ yard of the same fabric used for the warp (four 12½" x 12½" squares)

side two of napkins: ¾ yard of the same fabric used for the weft (four 12½" x 12½" squares)

contrasting fabric for napkin rings: ¼ yard (9" x 24" piece for four napkin rings)

water soluble stabilizer or muslin for base: ¼ yard

thread: use the same assorted threads as for placemats

water soluble basting thread

By Wendy Hill, Woven Placemats with Napkins & Napkin Rings

STEP 1

Pin two different napkin squares right sides together. Sew around the outside edge using a ¼" seam allowance, leaving a 2"–3" space open to turn the napkins. (Optional: curve the corner seams.) Trim the corners.

STEP 2

Turn the napkins right side out, using a pin to pick out the corners. Flatten the edges, pinning to hold flat, and folding in the seams along the opening. Hand sew the opening closed with a slip stitch. Press lightly; remove pins and press again well. Topstitch close to the edge.

STEP 3

For the napkin rings, stack the muslin or water soluble stabilizer base on the bottom with the fabric on the top. Pin or baste with water soluble thread. Surface stitch using pivots and wavy lines as I did, or your own combination of stitch styles. Wash and dry as usual. Cut the panel of surface-stitched fabric into four pieces, each 4½" x 6".

STEP 4

Fold each piece, with right sides together, into a rectangle, 2¼" x 6". Sew together along the 6" side with a ¼" seam, reinforcing both ends of the stitching line with back stitching.

STEP 5

Press seam open lightly; turn the tube right side out; press the tube flat so the seam runs down the middle of the back of the tube.

STEP 6

Pin the ends of the tube right sides together and sew with a ⅜" seam. Finger press the seam open. Add a little more surface stitching to hold the seam open, or lightly whip stitch the seam along the edges. Turn the napkin ring right side out.

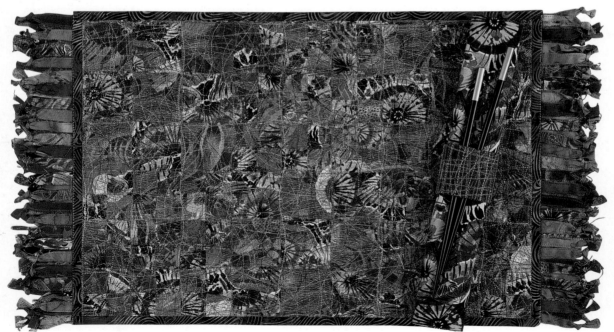

GIRL PILLOW

INSPIRATIONAL STARTING POINT

Method: collage using leftover surface-stitched fabrics

Stitch Style: assorted

April Hill (my mother-in-law) designed this pillow while visiting us. She began with a piece of fabric and an assortment of leftover pieces of surface-stitched fabric. Inspired by one bit of leftover surface-stitched fabric in particular, she built the girl around this one piece.

When finished arranging the design, the pieces were glued into place using fabric glue. I zigzagged around the edges with a narrow satin stitch using variegated thread, then added more fabrics to make a pillow top. Just because it is fun and easy to do, I added a contrast band across the back of the pillow, making the zipper flap. For those who like to see symbolism in their home decorator pillows, does the contrast band look like a picket fence (and therefore a happy life for the girl) or a railroad track (and a dream of escape)?

Designed by April Hill, made by Wendy Hill

Back of Pillow

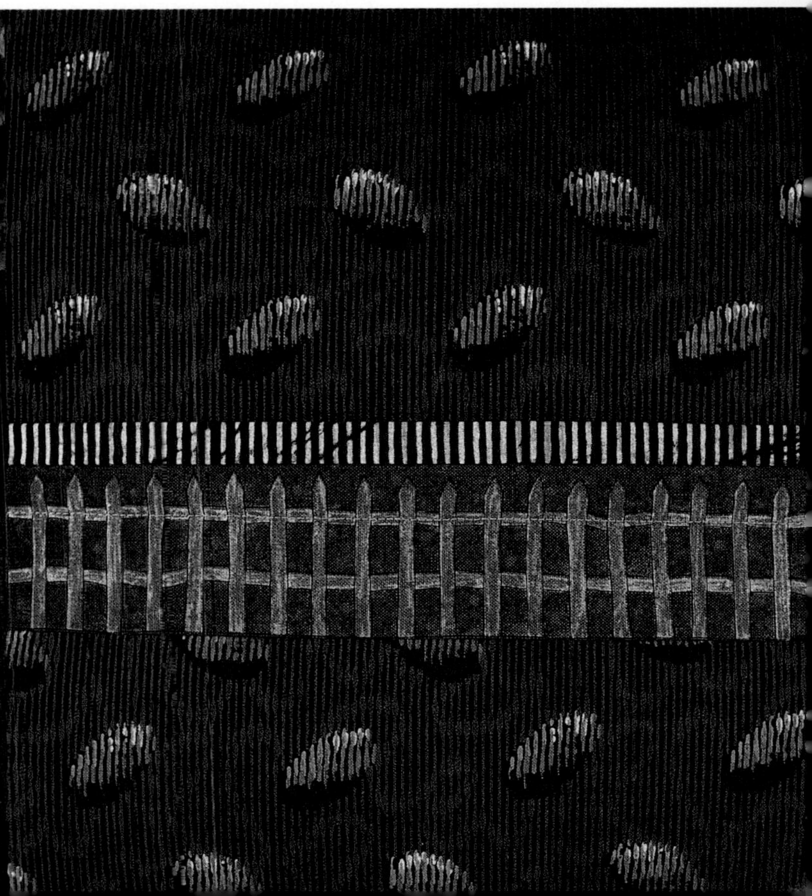

INSPIRATIONAL STARTING POINT

Method: whole cloth, raw-edge collage, weaving

We've seen these fabrics in Chapter 1, page 8, in a discussion on choosing a mix of fabrics. In Chapter 6, pages 57–63, an assortment of thread was added to the fabrics. Throughout Chapters 3, 4, and 5, we've seen these fabrics start to take shape with whole cloth, raw-edge collage, and weaving fabric manipulations. Now we see the finished pillows, a mix of surface-stitched and plain fabrics in an assortment of sizes and shapes.

To make your own bevy of pillows, purchase a commercial pattern or design your own patterns as I did. Use and adapt the methods shown in Chapters 3, 4, and 5 with your pillow patterns. Remember to add cording, binding, buttons, and extra design touches. To assist you in your pillow making, a brief discussion of each pillow follows.

Sharon Risedorph

Detail on page 6.

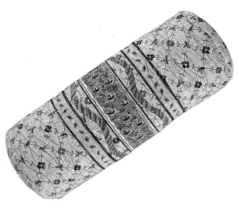

Details on pages 25 and 34.

Detail on pages 6.

FOUR CORNER PILLOW

I surface stitched a tiny red print fabric with an assortment of thread colors taken from the floral print (whole cloth). To reduce bulk, I used a water soluble stabilizer base, and finished off the triangles with a binding. The triangles are cut to overlap 1" past the center of each side and are included in the seam with the pillow back. The pillow back is finished with a flap and Velcro®.

CYLINDER PILLOW

I love the look of appliqué, but don't always have the time to do it. I cheated with this pillow by cutting up elements of a stripe fabric and appliquéing it to the rectangle of fabric (for the body of the cylinder) with a red piping. I used a ½" bias strip of the green fabric to make the wavy green accent between the striped panels. I surface stitched the big rectangle with a water soluble stabilizer. The pillow ends use unstitched fabric and the back closes with Velcro.

FOUR-FLAP PILLOW

This fun pillow is constructed with four lined flaps cut 2" shorter than the sides of the pillow dimensions. First, muslin triangles (cut 2" larger for shrinkage) were collaged with random shapes, surface stitched, washed, and dried. Next, each triangle was cut to size, lined, then bound with red, raw-edge, leftover surface-stitched fabric strips on the two inside edges. The triangles were laid out onto the pillow and pinned in place. The buttons were machine stitched through all the layers. The rest of the pillow was constructed as usual, with a flap and zipper in the back.

FACING PAGE: By Wendy Hill. From left to right: Woven Covered Pillow, Pillow with Flange, Cylinder Pillow, Four Corner Pillow, Fussy Cut Covered Pillow, and Four Flap Pillow

Details on pages 19 and 43.

Details on pages 52 and 55.

Detail on page 55.

FUSSY CUT COVERED PILLOW

This pillow is actually two parts: the inside, a basic pillow in a glossy chintz with a zipper in the back; and the outside, a one-piece cover slipped over the pillow.

The cover is made up of two pieces, the front and the back. The cover is the same height as the pillow dimension, but is narrower in width (about 4") than the pillow. Only the front is surface stitched over a wreath of fussy-cut floral motifs and free-cut leaf shapes from the textured green fabric. As an accent, the edges of the cover are bound in yellow.

PILLOW WITH FLANGE

This pillow looks far more complex than it really is. The pillow was "built" on a large piece of glossy chintz, cut the size of the pillow, plus the flange, plus 4" for shrinkage.

The center design is a square within a square, made with highly contrasting red and green fabrics. This surface was cut into strips (leaving the top edge intact), and woven with the same size strips cut from the multicolored floral fabric. The result is the illusion of seeing both the checkerboard and the square within a square at the same time.

I made ½" bias strips with most of my leftover fabrics. Loosely measuring, the strips were placed on the diagonal in both directions around the flange. The strips were woven (over, under), measured to be parallel from each other, and pinned in place. The top was basted, surface stitched, washed, and dried.

The raw edges between the center design and flange were covered with a ½" bias strip.

WOVEN COVERED PILLOW

The front and back of this pillow are made in one piece; a big rectangle cut to allow for shrinkage and zipper installation with a flap. I added two different contrasting fabrics along the sides.

Just the front of the pillow is woven (the back is left in one piece). I cut the blue-and-white plaid fabric on the bias, so the diagonal weaving would make a great contrast to the checkerboard print. I used the floral fabric cut the same width to weave the front. I scattered assorted sized spiral shapes and fat worm shapes in contrasting fabrics over the weaving, glueing them in place with a water soluble glue stick. I zigzagged all the raw edges, then surface stitched, washed, and dried as usual.

With a one-piece pillow cover, I inserted the zipper first. Then, with the weaving centered on the front, the side seams are sewn with the fabrics right side together. Remember to leave the zipper open a little bit so you have a way to turn the pillow right side out.

LIGHT-SWITCH COVERS

PROJECT

Method: whole cloth

Stitch Style: pivot; black and pastel with over-grid

I adapted an idea for customizing light-switch covers by using surface-stitched fabric, either leftovers or specially stitched for a room decor. My son Lucas surface stitched the fabric. It doesn't take much time to surface stitch the fabric, and the look of covered plates on the wall is sensational.

SUPPLIES

(Amounts given for one light-switch cover)

fabric or jewelry glue

lightweight cardboard: approximately 3" x 5"

surface-stitched fabric: approximately 5" x 6"

masking tape or narrow fabric strips, about ¼" wide x 1¼" long

STEP 1

Prepare the switch by cutting the cardboard to 2¾" x 4½". Check the fit with the light-switch cover. The cardboard should fit snugly against the back of the plate.

STEP 2

Cut a rectangular hole in the middle of the cardboard, large enough to allow access for the screws and switch when mounting the cover on the wall.

STEP 3

Lightly spread a little glue around the back edge of the cover plate. Press onto the cardboard, lining up the edges. It is okay to shift the cardboard around to line up the edges; just wipe off excess glue around the edges.

STEP 4

While the glue dries, or at least firms up, cut the surface-stitched fabric to 4" x 5¾".

STEP 5

Lightly spread the front of the switch cover with glue. Press onto the wrong side of the fabric, centering the switch. Gently stretch the fabric, smoothing it out across the front of the switch plate. Pull the excess fabric around to the back, and glue the fabric to the cardboard. Fiddle and adjust the corners to be smooth and rounded. Allow the glue to set up before continuing.

STEP 6

To finish the switch hole, cut a mirrored "Y" shape.

Lightly spread glue on the cut "Y" shape fabric and pull to the inside. This step is a little messy, but persevere. Use the narrow fabric strips to glue and hold these "facings" to the inside of the cover, or try using masking tape. Allow to dry thoroughly before mounting on the wall.

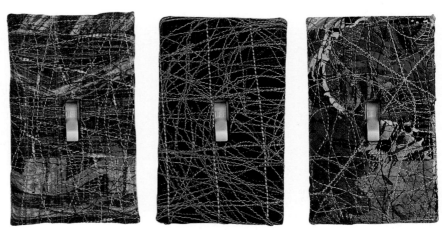

By Lucas Hill

SMALL PROJECTS

One-of-a-kind surface-stitched accessories may be easily added to your clothing and home. Plan ahead when making a piece of clothing; purchase extra fabric to make a surface-stitched accessory to match. This kind of style would be hard to purchase at any price. Save leftovers to make jewelry, greeting cards, and other small projects. Or take advantage of a free afternoon to make a magical tiny tote, a humorous soft sculpture or some other small delight.

BUTTON BABIES AND ERASER HEADS

PROJECT

Method: any method or leftovers

Stitch Style: assorted

An admirer of wearable-art jewelry, I have no jewelry experience and little time to learn a new craft. One day, while thinking of ways to use leftovers and mulling over the jewelry question, I invented these Button Babies and Eraser Head doll pins. Anyone can make these whimsical pieces of jewelry formed almost entirely of objects found around the house. Start saving your thread snips in a plastic bag strategically placed near the sewing machine for the hair.

I "kidnapped" two women from the parking lot of my son's school and "required" them to make the Button Babies and Eraser Head doll pins. Neither of them had ever made anything like it before. They were given the pattern, materials, and lots of encouragement to put their own individuality into the dolls. Soon each doll was emerging with its own personality, a modified cardboard shape, styled hair, and thoughtfully selected bead "shoes." I hope you have fun making your own doll pins created especially for your wardrobe or as fun gifts.

Designed by Wendy Hill, made by Robin Struthers, and Lila Krause

SUPPLIES

(Amounts given for one doll)

surface-stitched fabric: two 3" x 4" pieces

lightweight cardboard: approximately 3" x 4"

rattail cording: about 15" of rainbow or solid color

¾" button or pencil top eraser: bright colored

beads with holes: two with holes large enough for rattail cording to slip through

thread: snips for hair

masking or clear tape

pin back

fabric glue

STEP 1

Trace the doll pattern to make a template for the body. Trace the template onto the lightweight cardboard and cut out the body. Label the body front and back.

STEP 2

Place the front right side down onto the wrong side of the fabric; trace and cut out. Place the back right side down on the wrong side of the fabric; trace and cut out.

STEP 3

To make the arms and legs, cut a length of rattail cording (one piece for the arms and one piece for the legs), allowing extra for the knots. Wendy Hill doll pins feature short arms and long legs, but adjust the lengths to your liking. Knot the ends of the arms. Thread the beads onto the legs, and knot below the bead. You can also put a knot above the bead to hold it in place, but this is optional.

STEP 4

Place the arms and legs onto the back of the cardboard body. Hold in place with a small piece of tape.

STEP 5

Lightly spread glue onto the wrong side of the fabric body pieces. Matching the front piece of fabric with the front of the cardboard (and the back piece with the back), press the fabric onto the cardboard. Allow to dry.

STEP 6

For Button Babies, hand or machine sew a button onto the front of the doll, through all the layers. For Eraser Heads, trim the circular head to a rectangle as shown on the pattern piece. When the eraser is pushed onto the cardboard, it should be a tight fit. The only thing holding the eraser in place is the tight fit over the cardboard.

STEP 7

Style the hair from a collection of thread snips. (If you don't have a thread snip stash, unwind one or more threads to make a collection.) Include seam trimmings for bows and accents if desired. Make pony tails, bouffant, or just plain wild and crazy hair styles. When satisfied with the hair, use the fabric glue to attach it to the back of the head.

STEP 8

Glue a pin back onto the back of the doll, and you're ready to go out on the town.

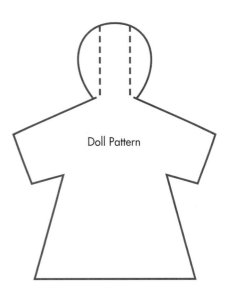

Doll Pattern

GREETING CARDS

Method: any, or use leftovers
Stitch Style: assorted

There are many ways to make your own greeting cards, using your own paper or purchased blank cards and envelopes.

One kind of purchased card comes with a precut opening in the front of the card. Usually this kind of card has three folds, with the extra fold to cover up the opening on the inside of the card. Make a special surface stitched scene, or use leftovers to place behind the cutout hole. If there is no extra flap, cut a piece of paper to cover the inside of the card for a more finished look.

Another way to use a blank card is to sew right on the paper of the card. Create a scene or abstract design with surface-stitched fabric, then sew the pieces to the card using a universal needle and any kind of thread. If your machine makes letters, add a stitched greeting to the card. Or instead of sewing right on the card, use glue to adhere the fabric pieces.

Combine surface-stitched fabric with other card making methods, such as embossing or rubber stamping. For inspiration, look at the kinds of cards available at a card store. Remember to make your own original work by combining your own ideas with the things you see. Think about making cards as a family project for birthdays, anniversaries, and any of the holidays throughout the year. Handmade cards are treasured by relatives and friends, and could end up being framed as keepsakes.

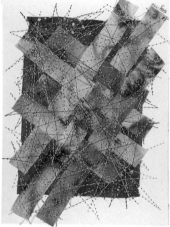

By Kelly Simbirdi

COFFEE COATS

Method: any, or use leftovers
Stitch Style: assorted

Heather Braley designed these little guards to use with her lattes and mochas. She agreed to make a few "coats" with leftover surface-stitched pieces of fabric. This is another example of the way virtually everything which can be made of fabric can be surface stitched first. What can you think of to make with a surface-stitched piece of fabric?

By Heather Braley, Caroline's Coffee Roasters, Grass Valley, California

TINY TOTES

Method: whole cloth

Stitch Style: pivot; Celestial tote: over-grid in star pattern

Laura Clark is a busy woman, so she wanted to make a special accessory in a short amount of time. These tiny totes, also called "penny purses" or "fairy totes," are a popular accent to wear around the neck. Laura used the whole-cloth method to make "new" fabric, then followed the pattern directions to make the totes. For the Celestial Tote Laura added an over-grid in gold metallic thread to form two starburst patterns in strategic locations. Instead of using silk ribbon embroidery on the felt penny purse, she added a collage of buttons, attached with a hot glue gun. (see Resources on page 141 for pattern information)

By Laura Clark; Celestial, Blue and Pink Floral pattern by Trinkets #CQ132, Country Quilter; purple felt pattern by Silk Ribbon and Felt Penny Purses #3097

WEARABLE-ART DOLLS

Method: using leftovers

Stitch Style: mixed assortment

Susie Uyeda, a wearable-art dollmaker, creates her own original designs and makes her dolls from scratch with love and attention to detail (see the Resources for ordering information). I asked Susie if she'd look at a few leftover surface-stitched fabrics and see if she'd be inspired to make one or two dolls. Indeed, she was inspired and challenged by the different weights of the fabrics (some had three layers) and her own time restrictions. Susie made seven dolls, each with its own personality.

To make your own dolls, create your own designs or use a purchased pattern.

By Susie Uyeda

THE POD

Method: whole cloth

Stitch Style: improvisational

Heather Braley is a fiber artist who makes "pods," or soft sculptures, among many other things. I asked her to make a surface-stitched pod, so she did. The pods are hollow, and can be hung by monofilament, or posed upright or sideways. Heather often displays a group of pods, in a variety of sizes, in clusters.

This is an example of how just about anything can be made using surface stitching. To make your own soft sculpture, create your own design or use a purchased pattern.

MINIATURE LANDSCAPE WALLHANGING

Method: raw edge collage using leftover surface stitched fabrics, with additional stitching through all the layers.

Stitch Style: improvisational

The United Parcel Service delivery man dropped off a package of surface stitched leftovers one afternoon, and one and one-half hours later Kelly Simbirdi had created this page-sized landscape.

Kelly likes to dive into projects without thinking too much, a strategy which works very well for her.

Kelly started with a backing fabric and muslin middle layer. She cut up the leftover surface stitched fabrics into random shapes and collaged them over the muslin. She let the colors and textures lead the way, and this sunset-over-water emerged. Kelly pin basted, but using a water soluble glue stick or a layer of water soluble stabilizer over the surface with a few pins would work too.

Kelly added more surface stitching to hold the layers in place. After washing and drying, she squared up the landscape, and tried a variety of things to finish the edges. Since she liked the look of the cut edges, Kelly zig-zagged a multi-colored yarn in place about ¼" from the edge with monofilament thread.

By Heather Braley

By Kelly Simbirdi, 11¾" x 12¾"

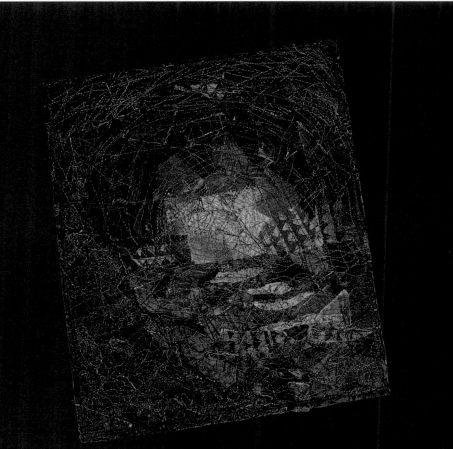

CLUTCH PURSE

Method: whole cloth

Stitch Style: pivot stitch

Heather made this purse to go with her dress, shown on page 106.

She used the same cotton and rayon fabric, with reverse appliqué. The purse could be used alone, but it adds a designer touch to have a purse to match the dress for a more formal look.

To make your own purse, create your own pattern, as Heather did, or use a commercial pattern. Use any method to create "new" fabric, then follow the directions to complete the purse. Try adding binding, cording, or other embellishment to make the purse with your own original flair.

SET OF COVERS FOR BOOKS, TISSUE, AND SUNGLASSES

Method: whole cloth or leftovers

Stitch Style: improvisational

Karla Rogers designed the covers to use herself or to make as fun gifts. She used the same fabric for all three, and surface stitched one big piece using a water soluble stabilizer. Develop your own pattern as Karla did, or see the Resources on page 141 to order a pattern from Karla. She used a fat quarter (18" x 22" piece of fabric) to make all three items, but a smaller or larger book would change the fabric requirement.

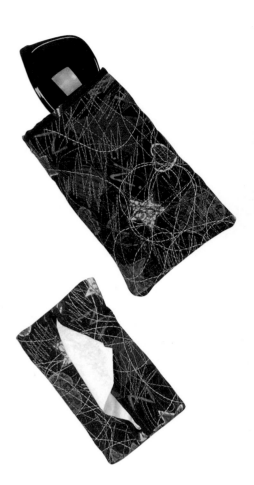

By Karla Rogers

By Heather Braley

MEET THE CONTRIBUTORS

FRAN ANDRE says she has "dyed, bleached, painted, marbleized, ripped, wrinkled, burned, quilted, crocheted, knitted, braided, spun, woven, recycled, and sewn fabric" in every imaginable way since her early childhood. Fran currently teaches art with developmentally handicapped adults in Grass Valley, California.

CHRISTINE BARNES is a free–lance writer, editor, and quilt teacher with degrees in journalism and design. Recent titles are *Color: The Quilter's Guide* and *Velda Newman: A Painter's Approach to Quilt Design.* Christine lives in Grass Valley, a historic mining town in the California gold country.

HEATHER BRALEY is a fiber artist, full-time student, mother, and wife. She has a studio in the Sierra Nevada mountains of California where she has taught sewing to both adults and children. She is especially interested in 3-D fiber art, and the potential of fiber in art therapy.

SANDRA BRUCE, from Grass Valley, California, enjoys traveling, gardening, collecting masks, experimenting with polymer clay, and making quilts, which she describes as a "wonderful form of self–expression." Sandra learned to sew at age seven on a treadle machine in Virginia, and began a career as a calligrapher/ illustrator in 1983.

LAURA CLARK, from Nevada City, California, works for Ben Franklin Crafts Store of Grass Valley as a craft coordinator and buyer. This job suits her love of trying new crafting techniques and teaching others through craft classes and demonstrations.

KAZUKO DAILEY, a resident of Nevada City, California, decided to try something different after retiring from her career as a library administrator. To her surprise, she found a good match for her life long interest in abstract art and her new attraction to quilting. Kazuko's work has been included in several exhibits since 1994.

KATE EDWARDS is a graphic designer who has enjoyed sewing and quilting most of her life. She recently illustrated a children's book in which all the artwork was done in fabric. A resident of Grass Valley, California, Katie enjoys just playing with fabrics on her own to create pieces which have no purpose whatsoever!

APRIL HILL is a painter and non-fiber artist living and working in Palo Alto, California.

LUCAS HILL from Sunriver, Oregon, made his first quilt (with help) when he was five years old and his second quilt at eight, in 1996. His favorite activities are watching television, playing with friends, and eating.

LORRAINE KELLEY, inspired by the open-ended technique classes taught by Wendy Hill, loves to work out color combinations and the intricate look of surface stitching using only very basic sewing skills. Lorraine lives with her husband in Nevada City, California, where she enjoys sewing, gardening, and visits from her many children and grandchildren.

DEDE LEUPOLD lives in Bend, Oregon. With experience in many art media over the past thirty years, she became interested in polymer clay in 1991. Her company, Bumblebeads, began as a home schooling project with her daughters as a way to teach business skills and nurture the creative side. Since then Dede has become known for her jewelry designs, receiving an award in 1996. Her work is widely shown in galleries and art shows. Dede lives with her husband Will, their two daughters Cora and Brooke (who are still involved in the business), three cats, and lots of beads.

CHARLOTTE PATERA, a graphic designer, was drawn to fibers early on. She took up appliqué and other needlework in the mid-60s, and since then has written numerous how–to articles for magazines as well as five books, including *Mola Techniques for Today's Quilters* and *Schoolhouse Appliqué, Reverse Techniques and More.* Her research into the Kuna Indian molas has influenced much of her appliqué work. Currently Charlotte is engaged in researching prehistoric rock art, which is the subject of most of her recent quilts.

SANDRA RADTKE lives in Bend, Oregon, with her husband. For over thirty years she has made clothing and quilt tops for herself and family, but in 1992 she discovered free-motion embroidery through the Machine Embroiderers of Oregon and Washington (MEOW). A certified machine embroidery instructor, Sandra works for a sewing machine dealer in Bend and teaches classes on the topics of machine use and embroidery.

KARLA J. ROGERS recently came home to her country roots after a move from southern California to a ten acre farm outside of Nevada City, California. Karla, who shares a love of needle arts with her mother, began quilting in 1972. In addition to belonging to the local quilt guild and work with the Junior Quilters, Karla lives with her husband, son, two dogs, two cats, two rabbits, two finches, chickens, an aquarium, and the newest additions—two kinder goats.

ANN SANDERSON says she has always been crazy about textiles. Following a degree in Clothing and Textiles twenty some years ago, Ann has followed a diverse path which includes teaching, exploring a variety of media, and free-lance photo styling, all of which have in common problem solving, attention to detail, and the creative process. Currently living in Nevada City, California, Ann's goal is to surround herself with inspirational people and give herself more time to do "her thing."

KELLY SIMBIRDI of San Carlos, California, started quilting "in hopes of putting some distance" between herself and the refrigerator during her second pregnancy. Fifty–five pounds later she was hooked, on quilting that is. Now back to her normal weight, Kelly currently teaches quilt classes on a variety of techniques.

ROBIN STRUTHERS and LILA KRAUSE were abducted from the school parking lot one morning and held hostage until they made Button Babies and Eraser Head wearable-art pins, with only a mound of supplies in front of them and a promise to be returned safely to their children by the end of the school day. Both women, who live in Sunriver, Oregon, said they had a wonderful time, considering the circumstances.

SUSIE UYEDA, a resident of Los Altos, California, is a full–time renal dietitian by day, and a wearable-art dollmaker by night. Susie says "creating these handmade works of art" is a way to relax from a hard day at work. The designs are original, with the fabrics personally selected by Susie, and made with love. With Susie's creative vision, she knows each will be "received with love and will be treasured keepsakes" for years to come.

SANDY WAGNER, who lives in Pine Grove, California, began sewing on a toy sewing machine as a young child. When she made her first quilt in 1979, Sandra says, "It was love at first sight." A former owner of her own quilt shop, Sandy is currently exhibiting her work in galleries and shows, teaching creative clothing techniques, and accepting commission work.

DEBRA WRUCK of Grass Valley, California, began going to fabric stores as a young child with family members who sewed. She didn't like sewing until she was forced to take a sewing elective her senior year in high school. She discovered a love for sewing that year, and later quilting. Debra still has a passion for fabrics, buttons, and thread, and says if there is a fabric store nearby, she'll "be sure to find it."

RESOURCES

There are several reasons to shop at independently owned stores, including good service and good quality products. Store owners have the time and knowledge to offer personal service and assistance. Since the owners want and need your repeat business, they will be sure to stand behind their products. Look or ask for these products at your local independent fabric, sewing, or quilt-related shop:

JEWELRY & BUTTONS

Bumblebeads
Dede Leupold
Polymer Clay Buttons and Jewelry
P.O. Box 9342
Bend, Oregon 97708
LSASE for color brochure
Dede combines the millefiori of the glass bead maker and the pattern-piecework of the quiltmaker in her jewelry. She concentrates mainly on detail in miniature designs. Bumblebeads is now offering a mail-order service. Custom work considered.

Susie Uyeda
Doll Jewelry, Kits, Hand-Painted T-Shirts
2133 Sierra Ventura Drive
Los Altos, California 94024
Phone: 415-965-0668
Fax: 415-961-2989
E-Mail: SusieU1942@AOL.com
Susie's creations may be purchased directly by mail from Susie.

MISCELLANEOUS MAIL ORDER

Cotton Patch Mail Order
3405 Hall Lane, Dept. CTB
Lafayette, California 94549
e-mail: cottonpa@aol.com
Phone: 1-800-835-4418
510-283-7883
A complete quilting supply store. Call or write for a catalog.

Karla Rogers
18251 Star Duster Drive
Nevada City, California 95959
Pattern for covers: book with handles, individual tissue package, and sunglasses case. Send LSASE and $4.00 for the three patterns.

Speedstitch, Inc.
3113 Broadpoint Drive
Harbor Heights, Florida 33983
Phone: 1-800-874-4115
All Sulky products available retail and wholesale by mail from Speedstitch, Inc. Send $3.00 for full catalog, refundable with first purchase.

YLI
P.O. Box 109
Provo, Utah 84603-0109
Phone: 1-800-854-1932
Call or write for the color sheets describing their line of quality sewing and embroidery products available retail and wholesale by mail from YLI, including water soluble thread (Wash-A-Way™), water soluble stabilizer (Solv-It ™), silk ribbon for embroidery, 100% silk thread (Kanagawa silk thread) and much more.

THREAD

American Effird Incorporated
Phone: 1-800-847-3235
Mettler 100% cotton embroidery (30 and 40 weight, 153 colors), 100% mercerized cotton (50 weight, 204 colors), and Metrosene 100% polyester (238 colors) and Signature™ All-Purpose Cotton Wrapped, Polyester Core Thread in 270 up-to-date, colorfast shades. Call for a distributor near you.

Coats and Clark
Consumer Service
P.O. Box 27067
Greenville, SC 29616
Manufacturer of Coats Dual Duty Plus®, Coats 100% Mercerized Cotton, Coats Dual Duty Plus for Overlock®, and Coats Specialty (Stitch n' Fuse™, nylon mono-filament, metallic, rayon, upholstery nylon) threads and Molynke 100% long fiber polyester thread. Write for a distributor near you.

Gütermann
8227 Arrowridge Boulevard
Charlotte, North Carolina, 28273
Phone: 704-525-7068
Hand and machine sewing threads; cone thread for sergers; and heavy duty topstitching, metallic, silk, upholstery, and cotton quilting threads. Call for a distributor near you.

Madeira
Madeira Division
SCS/USA
Phone: 1-800-547-8025
Madeira Division, SCS/USA, is the exclusive North American agent for the retail division of Madeira, Germany, and includes Madeira rayons, cottons, metallics, polyesters, serger, and embroidery threads, trims and other products for machine and hand decorative stitching. Call for free catalog of all Madeira and other products available for retail sales.

Speedstitch, Inc. (Sulky of America)
3113 Broadpoint Drive
Harbor Heights, FL 33983
Phone: 800-874-4115
Manufacturer of rayon (30 weight, 102 colors and 40 weight, 231 colors), original metallic (36 colors), Sliver Metallic™ (24 colors) threads and other products. All Sulky products available by mail from Speedstitch, Inc. Send $3.00 for a full catalog (refundable with purchase).

PATTERNS

Look for these patterns in your favorite stores. If you can't find what you are looking for, contact the appropriate company listed below.

Color Me Patterns
By Shirley Fowlkes
Old Indian Creek Ranch
1617 Bear Creek Road
Kerrville, Texas 78028
Phone: 210-367-2514
Call or write for a catalog. (Bubble Wrap Jacket pattern #202)

Country Quilter
Routes 100/102
Somers, New York 10589
Phone: 914-277-4820
(Tiny Totes - Celestial Floral, Trinkets #CQ132)

Design Originals
2425 Cullen Street
Forth Worth, TX 76107
1-800-877-7870
(Tiny Totes - Felt, Silk Ribbon & Felt Penny Purses #3097)

Fashion Blueprints
2191 Blossom Valley Drive
San Jose, CA 95124
Phone: 408-356-5291
(Fashion Blueprints #402)

Folkwear
The Taunton Press
63 S. Main Street
Box 5506
Newtown, CT. 06470-5506
Phone: 1-800-888-8286
Call or write for a distributor near you. (Afgani Nomad pattern)

Ghee's
2620 Centenary Boulevard #2-250
Shreveport, Louisiana 71104
Phone: 318-226-1701
Call or write for a free catalog of patterns, books, and handbag accessories. (Linda's Vest #693)

k.p. kids & company
Route 1, Box 13
Fairfield, Washington 99012
Phone: 509-291-6060
Call or write for a retail catalog. (Blooming Baby Boutique—Kids Jumper Overalls, Wild West Jumpers —Adult Jumper w/ Tiered Skirt)

Timber Lane Press
North 22700 Rimrock Road
Hayden Lake, Idaho 83835
Phone: 208-765-3353
Call or write for a catalog of patterns. (Kaleidoscope Cap #204)

Log Cabin Dry Goods
East 3445 French Gulch Road
Coeur d' Alene, Idaho 83814
Phone: 208-664-5908
Call or write for a catalog of patterns and other products.

Park Bench Pattern Company
Mary Lou Rankin
P.O. Box 837
Longmont, Colorado 80502-0837
Phone: 303-772-5746
Fax: 303-772-5728
Send a check for $3.00 for a full catalog of patterns.

The Sewing Workshop
Linda Lee
2010 Balboa Street
San Francisco, California 94121
Phone: 415-221-7397
Call or write for a free catalog of patterns and ordering information. (Haiku Jacket, Hong Kong Vest and Panel Pants, and Bamboo Shirt)

INDEX

MEET THE AUTHOR

Wendy began sewing doll clothes around age six with the encouragement, if not exactly help, from her mother, who hated sewing. Under the guidance (or dictatorship) of a perfectionist home economics teacher, Wendy learned to employ professional tailoring techniques in high school. These skills were immediately applied to making a vinyl bikini swimsuit, a bright blue fake fur car coat, and a bread wrapper raincoat, which the sewing teacher evaluated highly for technical skill, if not good fashion judgment.

Wendy became a self–taught quilter in 1971 through common sense and the helpful hints found on Mountain Mist® batting wrappers. She used traditional patterns with her own color schemes, and always hand quilted. Thoroughly isolated from the larger quilt world until 1987, but well grounded in traditional quilting methods, Wendy turned to using an eclectic assortment of techniques to make her ideas come to life. Her technical skill and color sense are highly regarded among a broad range of quilters and fiber artists.

She attributes her love of color and design to a grandmother she never met, a gift sent to her through maternal genes. Wendy feels a strong kinship with this woman, who lived in rural Michigan in the early 1900s.

Wendy brought thirteen years of public schoolteaching experience to the development of a variety of open-ended quilt and surface design classes. Accustomed to designing curriculum for a wide range of ages and abilities in her classroom, Wendy is very comfortable leading classes for quilters with a mixture of interests and skill levels.

Wendy currently fills the roles of wife, mother, quilt artist, author, and teacher. Her quilts continue to be exhibited widely and published in books and magazines.

OTHER FINE BOOKS FROM C&T

An Amish Adventure—2nd Edition, Roberta Horton

Anatomy of a Doll, The Fabric Sculptor's Handbook, Susanna Oroyan

Appliqué 12 Easy Ways! Elly Sienkiewicz

Art & Inspirations: Ruth B. McDowell, Ruth B. McDowell

Art & Inspirations: Judith Baker Montano, Judith Baker Montano

The Art of Silk Ribbon Embroidery, Judith Baker Montano

The Artful Ribbon, Beauties in Bloom, Candace Kling

Baltimore Beauties and Beyond , Vol I, Elly Sienkiewicz

Basic Seminole Patchwork, Cheryl Greider Bradkin

Beyond the Horizon, Small Landscape Appliqué, Valerie Hearder

Buttonhole Stitch Appliqué, Jean Wells

Christmas Traditions From the Heart, (2 Volumes), Margaret Peters

Colors Changing Hue, Yvonne Porcella

Crazy Quilt Handbook, Judith Montano

Crazy Quilt Odyssey, Judith Montano

Crazy with Cotton, Piecing Together Memories & Themes, Diana Leone

Dimensional Appliqué—Baskets, Blooms & Baltimore Borders, Elly Sienkiewicz

Elegant Stitches, An Illustrated Stitch Guide & Source Book of Inspiration, Judith Baker Montano

Enduring Grace, Quilts from the Shelburne Museum Collection, Celia Y. Oliver

Everything Flowers, Quilts from the Garden, Jean and Valori Wells

The Fabric Makes the Quilt, Roberta Horton

Faces & Places, Images in Appliqué, Charlotte Warr Andersen

Fantastic Figures, Ideas & Techniques Using the New Clays, Susanna Oroyan

Fractured Landscape Quilts, Katie Pasquini Masopust

From Fiber to Fabric, The Essential Guide to Quiltmaking Textiles, Harriet Hargrave

Heirloom Machine Quilting, Harriet Hargrave

Imagery on Fabric, 2nd Edition, Jean Ray Laury

Impressionist Palette, Gai Perry

Impressionist Quilts, Gai Perry

Kaleidoscopes & Quilts, Paula Nadelstern

Landscapes & Illusions, Joen Wolfrom

The Magical Effects of Color, Joen Wolfrom

Mariner's Compass, An American Quilt Classic, Judy Mathieson

Mariner's Compass Quilts, New Directions, Judy Mathieson

Mastering Machine Appliqué, Harriet Hargrave

Nancy Crow, Improvisational Quilts, Nancy Crow

The New Sampler Quilt, Diana Leone

Papercuts and Plenty, Vol. III of Baltimore Beauties and Beyond, Elly Sienkiewicz

Patchwork Persuasion, Fascinating Quilts From Traditional Designs, Joen Wolfrom

Patchwork Quilts Made Easy, Jean Wells (co-published with Rodale Press, Inc.)

Pattern Play, Creating Your Own Quilts, Doreen Speckmann

Pieced Clothing Variations, Yvonne Porcella

Pieces of an American Quilt, Patty McCormick

Plaids and Stripes, Roberta Horton

Quilts for Fabric Lovers, Alex Anderson

Quilts from the Civil War, Nine Projects, Historic Notes, Diary Entries, Barbara Brackman

Quilts, Quilts, and More Quilts! Diana McClun and Laura Nownes

Recollections, Judith Baker Montano

Say It With Quilts, Diana McClun and Laura Nownes

Schoolhouse Appliqué, Reverse Techniques and More, Charlotte Patera

Simply Stars, Quilts that Sparkle, Alex Anderson

Six Color World, Color, Cloth, Quilts & Wearables, Yvonne Porcella

Small Scale Quiltmaking, Precision, Proportion, and Detail, Sally Collins

Soft-Edge Piecing, Jinny Beyer

Start Quilting with Alex Anderson, Six Projects for First-time Quilters

Stripes in Quilts, Mary Mashuta

Symmetry, A Design System for Quiltmakers, Ruth B. McDowell

3 Dimensional Design, Katie Pasquini

Tradition with a Twist, Variations on Your Favorite Quilts, Blanche Young and Dalene Young Stone

Trapunto by Machine, Hari Walner

A Treasury of Quilt Labels, Susan McKelvey

Visions: QuiltArt, Quilt San Diego

The Visual Dance, Creating Spectacular Quilts, Joen Wolfrom

Willowood, Further Adventures in Buttonhole Stitch Appliqué, Jean Wells

88 Leaders in the Quilt World Today, Nihon Vogue

For more information write for a free catalog from:
C&T Publishing, Inc.
P.O. Box 1456
Lafayette, CA 94549
(1-800-284-1114)
http://www.ctpub.com